BRITAIN
from the air

IAN HAY

Text by
GRAHAM PRITCHARD

MYRIAD

LONDON

First published in 2008 by
Myriad Books Limited
35 Bishopsthorpe Road,
London SE26 4PA

Photographs copyright ©
Ian Hay
Text copyright © Graham
Pritchard

ISBN 1 84746 131 X
EAN 978 1 84746 131 5

Designed by Jerry Goldie
Graphic Design
Printed in China

www.myriadbooks.com

Right: Sunderland; far
right: Caernarfon Castle;
title page: St Sunday Crag,
Lake District

CONTENTS

INTRODUCTION

The island of Britain is a remarkable mix of ancient and modern, natural and man-made. As humans we tend to see the sights from ground level or perhaps climb to the top of a hill or a building to admire them. Here is a fresh take on the riches that are scattered the length and breadth of Britain: from a bird's eye view you can see a whole new perspective and extraordinary detail.

Surely one of the great mysteries is Stonehenge (opposite): how did our ancestors bring the huge stones from far away to create the outer ring in an almost perfect circle? No one really knows, but 4,000 years later it remains a phenomenal achievement.

To the north, on Tyneside, the 1990s saw the installation of Antony Gormley's imposing Angel of the North statue (below). From the air you certainly appreciate it differently – its wings are almost as wide as those of a Jumbo jet.

In the intervening centuries some of the country's finest castles were built, such as Harlech Castle in north Wales. When you see this from above you appreciate that its design was its strength. You also get a feel for the symmetry and splendour of the architects' achievements in stately homes such as Harewood House in Yorkshire, and Hampton Court on the outskirts of London.

Nature has played its part in shaping Britain: it has given us the superb unspoilt regions of the Lake District in north-west England, Scotland's lochs and Snowdonia in north Wales. Human endeavours have produced rather more mixed results. Contrast the splendour of Britain's cathedral cities of York, Salisbury and Canterbury, and the ancient university cities of Oxford and Cambridge, with the starker legacy of industrial sites such as Port Talbot in south Wales, the docks at Immingham in eastern England or the china clay pits near Dartmoor.

Human impact has also had some unintended results, such as the colourful patterns of containers stacked up on the quayside in Felixstowe in eastern England. The intricate road pattern of Spaghetti Junction in Birmingham or the biodomes at Cornwall's Eden Project take on a new symmetry when seen from above.

From high up, hillside figures such as the Long Man of Wilmington, the Kilburn White Horse and the Cerne Abbas giant in Dorset come into their own in the modern era. And the logic behind the nicknames that newer landmarks have acquired becomes obvious: Paddy's Wigwam in Liverpool, the Doughnut in Cheltenham, the Gherkin in London and the Armadillo in Glasgow!

Britain is fringed by many miles of superb coastline, with fabulous beaches and spectacular natural phenomena: Chesil Beach in Dorset, Blackpool Beach in Lancashire and Flamborough Head in Yorkshire to name a few. With a nod to the poet William Blake, we can truly say that, viewed from above, Britain is a green and pleasant land.

Graham Pritchard

PART ONE

LONDON

Britain's capital, its seat of government, a major financial centre and home to the royal family, London is one of the world's greatest cities. Visitors flock here for its remarkable buildings, great green spaces, ceremonial pageantry and fascinating mix of people. Samuel Johnson's lines written over 200 years ago still ring true today: "When a man is tired of London, he is tired of life; for there is in London all that life can afford."

PALACE OF WESTMINSTER

Although Henry VIII moved out in 1512, Westminster (below) is still officially a royal palace. The oldest part of today's Houses of Parliament, Westminster Hall, dates from 1097. The present building was designed by Sir Charles Barry and completed in 1870. It is one of the world's largest parliaments, with almost 1,200 rooms, 100 staircases and over 2 miles (3km) of corridors. At the north-eastern end, close to Westminster Bridge, stands the 316ft (96m) tall Clock Tower, better known as Big Ben. This is in fact the name of the largest of the tower's five bells, which chimes every hour.

BUCKINGHAM PALACE

Buckingham House, the forerunner of today's palace
(above), was bought for Queen Charlotte by George
III in 1761 and became known as the Queen's House.
Remodelling and enlarging soon began. Three weeks
after Victoria came to the throne in 1837 she declared
the palace the official London residence of the
monarch. In front of the palace stands the white
marble Victoria Memorial erected in 1911.

Today's Buckingham Palace has 775 rooms. Every
year in August and September the 19 State Rooms are
open to the public. Spectators flock to see the daily
ceremony of the Changing of the Guard in the palace
forecourt.

WHITEHALL

Running between Trafalgar Square and Parliament
Square, Whitehall (right) has become synonymous
with "the Government". The street is lined with
government departments including the Ministry
of Defence, the Foreign and Commonwealth Office,
the Scottish and Welsh Offices and the Treasury.
Every year on Remembrance Sunday members of
the royal family join politicians, dignitaries and old
soldiers to remember the fallen at the Cenotaph.
It bears the simple words "The Glorious Dead".
A recent addition to Whitehall, the national
monument to the women of the Second World
War, was unveiled by the Queen in 2005.

WESTMINSTER ABBEY

Deriving its name from "west minster" (to differentiate it from the "east minster", St Paul's Cathedral) Westminster Abbey (left) was consecrated in 1065. It has been used for the coronation of every British monarch since 1066 except Edward V and Edward VIII. The present abbey is one of the country's most important Gothic buildings and dates from 1245. As a "Royal Peculiar", it does not belong to a diocese but to the monarch.

The setting for many royal weddings, the Abbey is also the burial place of kings and queens and key writers, musicians, scientists and politicians.

PORTCULLIS HOUSE

When it was commissioned in 1992, it was intended that controversial Portcullis House (above) would accommodate 210 Members of Parliament and their staff at a cost of £165m. Nine years later the final bill came to £235m, including £150,000 for fig trees in the central courtyard and a £440 reclining chair for each MP.

TRAFALGAR SQUARE

Nelson's Column dominates Trafalgar Square (above), named after the battle where Nelson defeated Napoleon's navy. The memorial, 185ft (56m) high, is topped with a 17ft (5m) high statue of the admiral. Four bronze lions by Sir Edwin Landseer guard the base of the column, and Sir Edwin Lutyens' large fountains gently play. To the north, the area in front of the National Gallery has been traffic-free since 2003. Statues commemorate a king and two generals on three plinths, while the fourth is an exhibition space for sculpture.

Whitehall Place (left) is lined with ministerial and government offices and connects Whitehall with the Embankment.

VICTORIA AND ALBERT MUSEUM

The V&A (right) was established in central London
in 1852 as the Museum of Manufacturers, a legacy from
the 1851 Great Exhibition. Six years later it moved to South
Kensington. In 1899 Queen Victoria laid the foundation
stone for the building we see today at her last ever public
engagement, when the museum officially became the
Victoria and Albert Museum. One hundred and forty-five
galleries cover 11 acres and house over four million items
of decorative art and design from all over the world. The
plan to build the Spiral, Daniel Libeskind's controversial
extension, was shelved in 2004.

MARBLE ARCH

Marble Arch (below) has stood at the junction of Park Lane
and Oxford Street since 1851. It was originally designed by
John Nash in 1828 to serve as a gateway from the Mall to
Buckingham Palace. Only the King's Troop of the Royal
Horse Artillery and the royal family were allowed to pass
beneath. In the past, the spot where the arch now stands was
known as Tyburn. Until 1783 crowds would gather to witness
public executions at the three-legged gallows here. Across
the road at Speaker's Corner, in the north-east corner of
Hyde Park, people come to discuss every subject under the
sun on Sundays.

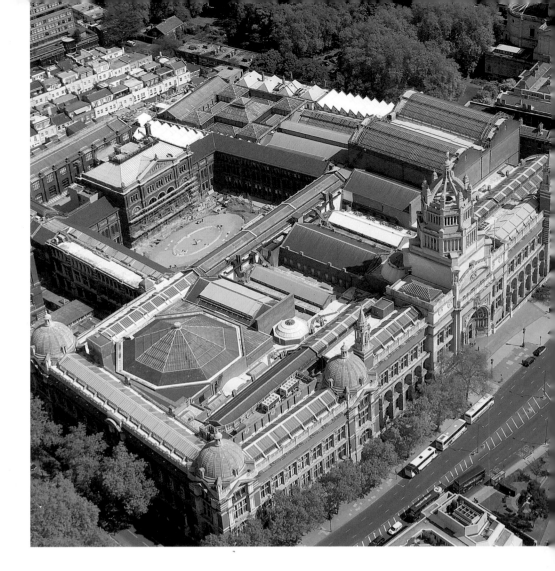

ROYAL ALBERT HALL

Queen Victoria opened the Royal Albert Hall of Arts and Sciences (right) in 1871. As with the Albert Memorial, opposite, in Kensington Gardens, it is dedicated to her husband, the Prince Consort. In the past the hall could accommodate audiences of up to 9,000, but modern safety regulations limit the present capacity to 5,544.

The venue is home to the BBC Proms, an annual series of summer concerts, and it also hosts many sporting events and pop concerts. When ABBA gave two concerts in 1977, the box office reportedly received 3.5m ticket requests.

REGENT STREET (NORTH)

Named after the Prince Regent (who became King George IV in 1820), Regent Street (left) was built by the great architect of London John Nash (1752-1835). He created a masterplan for this part of the town stretching north from Regent Street to Regents Park, and which included elegant terraces, crescents and shopping streets. Today Regent Street is one of the busiest in London, where the great names of Liberty and Hamleys jostle with the latest brands of Apple and Swarovski.

Upper Regent Street is the home of Broadcasting House, the headquarters of the BBC. The Oxford Circus tube station, where Regent Street crosses Oxford Street, is one of the busiest on the London Underground system.

PICCADILLY CIRCUS

Piccadilly Circus (left) was laid out in 1819 to connect Regent Street with Piccadilly. Some accounts say the name comes from *pickadil*, a type of broad lacy collar, others that it was a round hem or additions to a skirt hem. Away from the streaming traffic, set to one side of Piccadilly Circus, the Shaftesbury Monument memorial fountain commemorates the work of the Victorian philanthropist Lord Shaftesbury. The Angel of Christian Charity statue which graces the fountain is better known as Eros. It was the world's first statue cast in aluminium. The vibrantly illuminated advertising hoardings above shops on the north side have long been a popular tourist attraction, particularly at night.

ST JAMES'S SQUARE

St James's Square (below), one of London's first squares, dates from the 1670s and soon became one of the capital's most desirable addresses, home to seven dukes and seven earls. During the Second World War General Eisenhower and General de Gaulle both had their military headquarters here. Today the Georgian and neo-Georgian buildings largely house exclusive gentlemen's clubs and the offices of multinational companies.

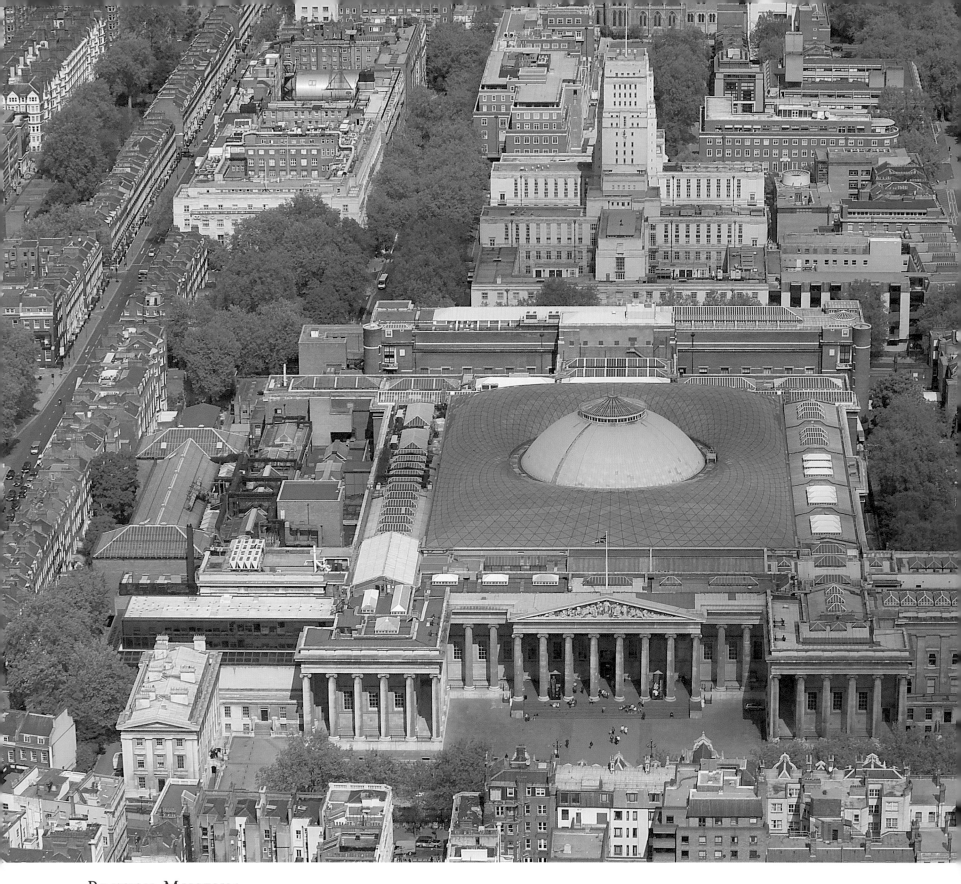

BRITISH MUSEUM

Every year the British Museum (above), one of the world's finest, attracts more than five million visitors. It was established by Act of Parliament in 1753 and first opened its doors in Montagu House in 1759. But a new home was needed to accommodate the growing collections, and between 1823 and 1847 the museum became Europe's largest building site while Sir Robert Smirke's neo-classical building took shape. When the British Library moved to its new purpose-built home in St Pancras in 1998,

Smirke's original courtyard was redeveloped. It opened two years later as the Queen Elizabeth II Great Court, surrounding the central Reading Room and designed by Sir Norman Foster. It is the largest covered square in Europe, with a roof made of 1,656 individually shaped glass sections. Controversy rages, however, over some of the museum's exhibits. Greece continues to demand the restitution of the Elgin Marbles and Nigeria the return of the Benin Bronzes.

BT TOWER

A tower of many names, the 620ft (188m) structure known today as the BT Tower (right) was first called the Post Office Tower and then the London Telecom Tower. It was officially opened by Prime Minister Harold Wilson in 1965. The following year the general public could go up to admire London from the viewing platforms or enjoy a meal in the restaurant on the 34th floor, which rotated once every 22 minutes. After a bomb exploded in the men's toilets in 1971 the restaurant (and subsequently the whole tower) was closed to the public for security reasons.

ROYAL COURTS OF JUSTICE

The Royal Courts of Justice (below) house the Court of Appeal and the High Court. The building was designed by the architect George Edmund Street. Construction began in 1873 but completion was delayed by industrial disputes, during which workers were brought in from abroad. Queen Victoria eventually opened the building in 1879. To fund the construction, £700,000 of the building costs were obtained by the court from the estates of people who had died leaving no will.

Swiss Re Building

Number 30 St Mary Axe (below) has firmly established itself in the hearts of Londoners as the Gherkin. It is also known as the Swiss Re building, after its main tenant, a Swiss reinsurance company. It occupies the site of the former Baltic Exchange, destroyed by an IRA bomb in 1992. Foster and Partners designed it as the city's first environmentally sustainable tower with 40 floors rising 590ft (180m). Those who work in the building and their guests can enjoy superb panoramic views from the tower's top floor bar. The Gherkin has won numerous awards, including the prestigious RIBA Stirling Prize when it opened in 2004.

Tower 42 (foreground) takes its shape from the logo of its original tenant, the NatWest Bank. At 600ft (183m) it was the UK's highest building until it was surpassed in 1990 by the towering Canary Wharf down river in Docklands.

St Paul's Cathedral

The Great Fire of London in 1666 destroyed the previous cathedral, and Sir Christopher Wren was brought in to design the fourth to occupy this site. He had been an architect for just three years when it was commissioned. By the time St Paul's (above) was finished he was 35 years older. One of London's greatest landmarks, Wren's splendid cathedral has been used for the funerals of Lord Nelson, the Duke of Wellington and Sir Winston Churchill and in 1981 for the wedding of Prince Charles to Lady Diana Spencer.

POOL OF LONDON

The section of the Thames known as the Pool of London (above) flows from Butler's Wharf and St Katherine Docks below Tower Bridge to London Bridge. Either side of this stretch of the river lie landmarks such as the Tower of London (founded in 1078) and Sir Norman Foster's elliptical City Hall, home of the Greater London Authority since 2002. Moored in the river is the museum ship *HMS Belfast*, which saw action during the Second World War.

TOWER BRIDGE

More than 70,000 tons of concrete and 11,000 tons of steel went into the construction of Tower Bridge (right) which started in 1886 and lasted eight years. Since 1974 the bridge's opening mechanism has been electro-hydraulically driven. It opens more than a thousand times a year, and each opening takes just a minute. As the Bridgemaster's Dining Room is now licensed for weddings and civil partnerships, it is possible to get married at Tower Bridge.

THE ISLE OF DOGS

Between Limehouse Reach and North Greenwich the Thames loops around the part of London known as the Isle of Dogs (above). Dockyards and shipyards thrived here from the early 1800s until the advent of container shipping forced their closure in 1969. Regeneration in the 1980s and 1990s brought about a new Docklands: today it is full of high-rise, high-tech business accommodation and waterside living space. The glass and concrete buildings of Canary Wharf contrast starkly with the Royal Naval College, Sir Christopher Wren's Baroque masterpiece on the south bank, at the centre of the Maritime Greenwich World Heritage Site.

The largest structure of its kind in the world, the Millennium Dome (right) was the focus for national celebrations for the new millennium in 2000. Designed by Sir Richard Rogers and supported by 12 328ft (100m) tall pylons, the Dome was surrounded by controversy, both political and financial, and visitor numbers fell well below expectations.

In 2005 the Dome was officially rebranded the O2, an entertainment complex housing an 11-screen cinema, exhibition space, the 20,000-seater O2 arena and almost 600 toilets.

CANARY WHARF

At the heart of Canary Wharf sits the UK's tallest inhabited building. Number 1 Canada Square, the 771ft (235m) tower, is better known as Canary Wharf. It was designed by the architect César Pelli and completed in 1991. Its triangular roof can be seen from miles around. In 2002, using only his hands and feet and with no safety equipment, the French urban climber Alain Robert scaled the outside of the building. Flanking Number 1 Canada Square are the UK's joint second highest buildings, both 654ft (199m) tall – Citigroup Centre and 8 Canada Square, also called the HSBC Tower.

HAMPTON COURT

When Thomas Wolsey, later Lord Chancellor and Cardinal, leased Hampton Court Palace (left) on the banks of the Thames in 1514, he set about making it a palace fit for a king. He gifted the palace to Henry VIII in 1525 but four years later he fell from grace after failing to have Henry's marriage to Catherine of Aragon annulled. In 1689 William III commissioned Sir Christopher Wren to redesign the King and Queen's apartments; his magnificent South Wing overlooks the formal gardens. The famous Maze was planted in 1691.

After the death of George III, Hampton Court was no longer a royal residence and Queen Victoria opened it to the public in 1838.

WINDSOR CASTLE

For nearly 1,000 years Britain's monarchs have lived at Windsor Castle (right). It is the oldest and the largest occupied castle in the world. In November 1992 nine of the castle's main rooms were destroyed by fire and many more were damaged. The five-year programme of restoration was partly funded by the opening of parts of Buckingham Palace to the public for the first time. Ten kings lie buried in the castle's St George's Chapel, along with Queen Elizabeth the Queen Mother and her daughter, Princess Margaret.

PART TWO

SOUTH-EAST ENGLAND

For many visitors, the south-east is the first part of the country they see – but it is often glimpsed fleetingly as they speed by car or train towards London. Were they to pause for a while, they would be rewarded with a kaleidoscope of views and experiences. Kent, the oldest county in England, with a proud historical heritage is known as the Garden of England where the white-painted chimneys of oasthouses peek out above sleepy apple orchards. Beautiful Sussex, with its rolling downs, offers traditional seaside fun – but often with a modern touch. And further along the coast, Hampshire's impressive naval heritage contrasts with the New Forest (despite its name, one of the oldest in the country) where the ancient landscape has remained unchanged for almost a thousand years.

QE2 BRIDGE

Part of the Dartford Crossing on London's M25 orbital motorway, the Queen Elizabeth II bridge (below) opened in October 1991. The central part of the cable-stayed bridge measures 1476ft (450m) and is suspended 213ft (65m) above the Thames to allow ships to pass beneath. Traffic crosses the bridge in a southbound direction; northbound traffic uses two tunnels under the river.

THAMES BARRIER

When central London last flooded in 1928, 14 people died. As tide levels in the Thames estuary were steadily rising, something had to be done to safeguard the city. The result was the Thames Barrier (above) which was completed in 1984. Its 10 separate moving gates span the 1700ft (520m) of the river at Woolwich. Each of the four main gates is 200ft (61m) wide, and when raised they can withstand a force of over 9000 tonnes. On the northern side of the river next to the barrier is the green space of the Thames Barrier Park.

DOVER AND THE CHANNEL TUNNEL

One of Edward the Confessor's Confederation of Cinque Ports, Dover (above) has been of strategic importance since the Romans knew it as *Portus Dubris*. Cross-Channel traffic really took off with the arrival of the railway in 1844. The most prestigious way to travel between London and Paris in the early 20th century was on the *Golden Arrow/Flèche d'Or* Pullman train. Even today, in the age of the plane, 14m passengers pass through Dover every year, and the port handles over 2m lorries. The Channel Tunnel (right) between Folkestone and Coquelles near Calais was officially opened by the Queen and the French President in May 1994. It is 31 miles (50.5km) long, of which 24 miles (39km) run under the English Channel, making it the world's longest undersea tunnel. Eurostar's passenger trains and Eurotunnel's car-carrying shuttle trains take just 35 minutes to pass through the tunnel.

CANTERBURY CATHEDRAL

Canterbury takes its name from *Cantwarebyrig*, old English
for "fortress of the men of Kent" and is dominated by its
cathedral. St Augustine, a missionary from Pope Gregory the
Great in Rome, founded it in 597AD. During the Middle Ages
and over the centuries it has been rebuilt in a variety of styles.

Henry II appointed his friend Thomas à Becket Archbishop
of Canterbury in 1162 but Becket vigorously defended the
church against royal intervention. Henry's rage at this
"meddlesome priest" prompted four knights to assassinate
Becket at the cathedral's altar in 1170. Three years later Becket
was declared a saint by the pope. Chaucer's *Canterbury Tales* of
1387 colourfully depict the antics of pilgrims on their journey
from London to the cathedral. One of the bawdiest of these
stories is *The Miller's Tale*.

Canterbury's cathedral, St Martin's (England's oldest church)
and the ruins of St Augustine's abbey are a World Heritage
Site. Dr Rowan Williams is the 104th Archbishop of
Canterbury and Primate of all England. He heads the Anglican
Communion, which has about 70m followers worldwide.

BLUEWATER

Europe's third largest shopping centre and leisure complex, Bluewater (left) opened in 1999 and is a cathedral to consumerism. It lies in a former chalk quarry, surrounded by 164ft (50m) high cliffs and is the size of 100 football pitches. The central shopping area has 330 retail outlets laid out over two floors and topped with glass-sided domes, enabling natural light to stream in.

McARTHUR GLEN

The architect Sir Richard Rogers has described his design for Ashford's McArthur Glen shopping centre (right) as "a Bedouin tent in an English meadow". Its purpose is rather more prosaic: an opportunity for retail therapy. Parking for 1450 cars is surrounded by an ovoid loop with more than 80 shops. The shopping area is covered by the world's longest continuous membrane structure, which extends over half a mile (1 km).

CHARTWELL

Overlooking the Weald of Kent, Chartwell (above) was the much-loved home of Sir Winston Churchill from 1922 until his death in 1965. The house began life as an Elizabethan manor house and takes its name from the Chart Well on the western edge of the estate. Churchill served for two periods as prime minister, from 1940-1945 and 1951-1955. Many consider him Britain's greatest politician of all time. During the 1930s, when the Conservative Party was out of office, Churchill devoted his time at Chartwell to writing. He called this period his "wilderness years", but they were not unproductive – he was awarded the Nobel Prize for Literature in 1953. Chartwell now belongs to the National Trust, and visitors can see Churchill's paintings and drawings, and visit his studio and the lovely gardens.

BEACHY HEAD

Beachy Head (above) is Britain's tallest chalk cliff, rising 530ft (162m) from the sea. Its name is derived from the French *beauchef* meaning "beautiful headland"; it is famous for its splendid views along the coast, and infamous for being a popular suicide spot.

When the lighthouse out at sea began operation in 1902 it was 541ft (165m) from the foot of the cliff. In 2001 part of the cliff known as the Devil's Chimney crashed into the water and this distance was reduced by more than half. Today the lighthouse is remotely operated.

THE LONG MAN

The origins of the Long Man of Wilmington (right) are sketchy. Europe's largest human hill figure is 227ft (69m) high, carved into the side of Windover Hill, north-west of Eastbourne. Some believe it is an ancient fertility symbol but archaeologists date it to the 16th or 17th century. In 1874 the figure was marked out by yellow bricks, which were painted green during the Second World War to prevent enemy aircraft using the figure for navigation. In 1969 the Long Man was renovated and its outline is now regularly painted to keep it visible from afar.

HASTINGS AND EASTBOURNE

Hastings (above) has long been associated with the famous battle of 1066. This bloody event took place to the north of Hastings at Senlac Hill now known as Battle. Every October a re-enactment attracts crowds of enthusiasts from all over the world.

Together with tourism, fishing has long been an important industry in Hastings, one of England's oldest fishing ports. On the Stade, the wide shingle beach, you can see Britain's biggest beach-launched fishing fleet of about 25 boats.

Eastbourne (left) boasts an unspoilt Victorian air with many seafront hotels facing its broad promenade. The pier was officially opened in 1870, but only completed two years later. It stretches some 1000ft (303m) out to sea. At the end of the pier you can now visit the dome and use the newly restored camera obscura, a 360° Victorian projector.

BRIGHTON

The little village of *Brighthelmston* was mentioned in the Domesday Book in 1086. Royalty started to visit Brighton (left) during the 18th century, and the Prince Regent (later King George IV) arrived in 1783. His summer residence, the Royal Pavilion, is the extravagant jewel in Brighton's crown. John Nash transformed the original farmhouse with his Indian-inspired design. Day-trippers from London thronged to the resort with the coming of the railway in 1841. Brighton's pebble beach (right) is one of the easiest to reach from the capital and its nickname is London-by-the-Sea. Today Brighton thrives as a centre for conferences and is a magnet for English language students.

NEWHAVEN FORT

When he was 22, Lieutenant John Charles Ardagh designed Newhaven Fort (below) to fit the contours of the surrounding land. Completed in 1871, it was the first military fortification to be built with concrete. The fort played an important role in the two world wars, but fell into disrepair. After much renovation, it re-opened in 1988 as a military heritage museum.

PORTSMOUTH

Most of Portsmouth (right and below) is located on Portsea
Island and it is the UK's only island city. It boasts a population
density second only to inner London and a naval heritage
second to none.

The town was founded by a Norman landowner, John de
Gisors, in 1180. Twenty years later a naval base was established
and the first docks built. For centuries, English monarchs
frequently used the base to attack the French and enhance
their naval power. In October 1805 Admiral Horatio Nelson
set sail aboard his flagship *HMS Victory* en route for his
famous victory over the French and Spanish at the Battle of
Trafalgar. Today *Victory* takes pride of place at Portsmouth's
Historic Dockyard (right). Built between 1759 and 1765, she is
the world's oldest warship still in commission. Nearby is the
splendid exhibition hall housing the *Mary Rose*, Henry VIII's
flagship which sank in 1545 and was raised in 1982. The city
celebrated its naval heritage in 2005 with the opening of the
558ft (170m) gleaming white Spinnaker Tower, in the shape of
a billowing sail. Southsea Common, facing the sea, has drawn
crowds to many a naval celebration, parade and aerial display.

ISLE OF WIGHT

With its mild climate, pretty villages and rugged coastline the Isle of Wight has always attracted visitors. Queen Victoria and Prince Albert would summer at Osborne House, and Charles Dickens, Lewis Carroll and Tennyson all came to the island. The pioneering photographer, Julia Margaret Cameron, lived at Freshwater Bay.

The Needles (above) are chalk stacks which stretch out to sea in the west of the island. The last lighthouse-keepers left in 1994 when the lighthouse was automated. In 1897 Guglielmo Marconi sent the first ever wireless transmission from a hotel on the colourful sandy cliffs of Alum Bay (right).

PART THREE

SOUTH-WEST ENGLAND

From Cornwall through Devon to Somerset, Dorset and Avon, the south-west has more than 600 miles of stunning coastline and 14 areas of outstanding natural beauty. So it's no surprise that all through the summer visitors flock to the area to visit such attractions as the stunning Eden Project and relax on the beaches. For walkers there are miles of footpaths and moorland to explore, while "end-to-enders" head straight to Land's End with one thing in mind: to walk or cycle the 874 miles from this southernmost tip of England to the most northerly point at John O'Groats in Scotland. The first person to complete this journey, Robert Carlyle, did it in 1879 pushing a wheelbarrow!

BOURNEMOUTH AND SANDBANKS

The seaside town of Bournemouth (above) was once nicknamed "God's waiting room" because of its ageing population. Today it is much more vibrant. More businesses in the resort applied for 24-hour drinking licences than anywhere else in the country and according to a 2007 online survey it is the happiest place in Britain. Seven miles (11km) of sandy beaches are lined with seafront gardens and clifftop hotels. Set back from the beach is the Bournemouth International Centre (bottom left of picture), a major venue for concerts and political party conferences. There has been a pier at Bournemouth since 1856 and it is still possible to catch a paddle steamer from the end of the pier to explore the Dorset coastline.

The beautiful Sandbanks peninsula (right) guards the entrance to Poole Harbour. It is rapidly becoming Britain's answer to the Florida Keys. Home to many celebrities, and with its main road nicknamed "Millionaire's Row", it has the fourth highest land values in the world.

STONEHENGE AND CERNE ABBAS

Take a moment to consider that the early earthworks at Stonehenge (above) date from around 3100BC; that the bluestones were brought 240 miles from south-west Wales to the site in about 2150BC; that the outer ring of sarsen stones, each weighing about 25 tonnes, arrived at Stonehenge about 150 years later – and there can be no doubt that Stonehenge deserves to be a World Heritage Site. Crowds still gather to celebrate the summer solstice though Stonehenge's original purpose remains a mystery.

The earliest written mention of the Cerne Abbas giant (right) dates from 1694, but his origin is unknown. The giant, also known as the Rude Man (meaning "naked man") is 180ft (55m) tall and 167ft (51m) wide, cut into a steep chalk hill north of Dorchester. He carries a 120ft (37m) long knobbly club, and is best seen from across the valley or from the air.

SALISBURY CATHEDRAL

Since its completion in 1320, this majestic cathedral (above) has dominated Salisbury. It has the UK's highest spire: 404ft (123m) tall. The superlatives continue: the cloisters are the largest in England, and the cathedral also owns what is probably Europe's oldest working clock, which dates from 1386. The octagonal Chapter House has one of the four remaining original copies of the *Magna Carta*, which dates from 1215.

WEYMOUTH

With a third more hours of sunshine than the rest of the country, Weymouth (above) has long been a popular holiday resort. King George III visited 14 times between 1789 and 1805. Outside the peak season, the town's wide sandy beach hosts a variety of sporting events including handball and beach volleyball. The international beach kite-flying festival in May regularly attracts over 40,000 spectators.

Weymouth's harbour today handles the biggest annual tonnage of fish in England and is also the point of departure for fast ferry services to St Malo in France and the Channel Islands.

SANDY BAY AND RED CLIFFS IN SOUTH DEVON

Serried ranks of holiday homes line the cliffs above the beach at Sandy Bay (above) close to Exmouth. It is at the end of the stretch of World Heritage Coastline known as the Jurassic Coast. Designated in 2001, the jagged red cliffs (below) to the east of Sidmouth are typical of the cliffs along this part of the coast, England's first natural heritage site. Stretching for 95 miles (153km) from the Old Harry Rocks near Swanage, walkers on the South-West Coastal Path can see at first-hand the breathtaking scenery of the Jurassic Coast.

CHESIL BEACH AND PORTLAND HARBOUR

It has been calculated that Chesil Beach (left) is made up of 180bn pebbles! The "tombolo" or shingle bank stretches 18 miles (28km) from Portland west towards West Bay; in parts it is 66oft (200m) wide and 5oft (15m) high. Behind it is the Fleet, a saltwater lagoon. This area is rich in wading birds, and at the Abbotsbury swannery hundreds of nesting mute swans rear their cygnets.

At the end of Chesil Beach rises the Isle of Portland (above), an important naval harbour since Henry VIII's time. The surrounding waters are classed as northern Europe's best by the Royal Yachting Association, so it is no surprise that the National Sailing Academy was established here on the south-western shore. Portland Harbour will stage the sailing events in the 2012 Olympic Games.

EXETER CATHEDRAL

The Cathedral Church of St Peter at Exeter (above) is a fine example of the Decorated Gothic architectural style. The cathedral was completed in 1369, although its sturdy Norman towers date from the 12th century. Above the nave soars the world's longest Gothic vaulted ceiling.

TORQUAY

During the Second World War wounded soldiers came to convalesce in Torquay (right). After the war the resort was promoted as a holiday destination. Today, with its palm-lined promenades, fine beaches and an excellent climate, Torquay lives up to its nickname of the English Riviera. The new marina, lined with popular bars and restaurants, can accommodate 440 boats.

DARTMOOR AND CHINA CLAY

Dartmoor National Park (left) covers an area of 368 square miles (953 sq km). Kaolin, or china clay, has been extracted from pits (right) south of Dartmoor since the 18th century; 75 per cent of the clay produced today is used in the paper industry as a coating, filler and whitener. A particular feature of Dartmoor are its large hills known as "tors" – there are over 160. Each May youngsters between the ages of 14 and 20 gather at Okehampton army camp for the Ten Tors Challenge: climbing 10 of these hills within two days. It is a tough proposition, as Dartmoor can be bleak and inhospitable.

DARTMOUTH NAVAL COLLEGE

The Britannia Royal Naval College, (right) overlooking Dartmouth, is the UK's only remaining naval training college. The town has been connected with officer training since 1863 when two training vessels were moored on the river Dart. The land-based college dates from 1905. Royal officer cadets to pass through Dartmouth include the Duke of Edinburgh, the Prince of Wales and the Duke of York.

PLYMOUTH

Overlooking Plymouth Sound, one of Europe's largest natural harbours, Plymouth (above) lies at the mouth of the Tamar and Plym rivers. It was one of the main departure points for the allied Normandy Landings in 1944. Today the port has more amicable ferry links with Santander in northern Spain and Roscoff in Brittany.

Sir Francis Drake reputedly played bowls on Plymouth Hoe (right) while waiting for the tides and winds to change, prior to defeating the Spanish Armada in 1588.

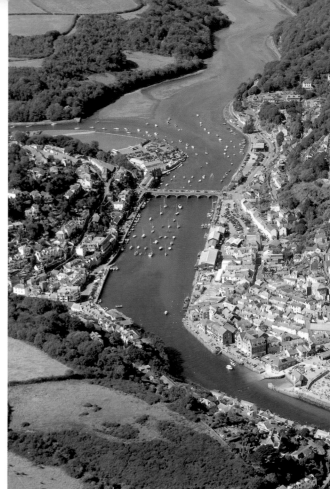

TAMAR BRIDGES

The river Tamar (above) forms a large part of the border between Devon and Cornwall. It is crossed by 20 bridges. The twin arches of Isambard Kingdom Brunel's Royal Albert Bridge, opened in 1859, carry the railway line across the river. When the Tamar road bridge (behind) opened in 1961 it was the UK's longest suspension bridge. Drivers have to pay a toll only when they leave Cornwall.

EDEN PROJECT

A hit since it opened in 2001, the spectacular Eden Project (right), the brainchild of Tim Smit, is sited in a former china clay pit near St Austell. The Humid Tropics Biome (foreground) is the world's biggest greenhouse and houses tropical plants. A Mediterranean climate has been created in the smaller Warm Temperate Biome, while the Outdoor Biome is planted with lavender, tea, hops and hemp.

CORNISH SEASIDE RESORTS

Looe (above left), on the river Looe, is rated as one of the 10 best places in Britain to celebrate the New Year. More generally the town thrives on tourism and fishing. The Shark Fishing Club of Great Britain is based here.

From JMW Turner to Barbara Hepworth, many of Britain's foremost artists have come to St Ives (above). Its importance in the nation's art scene was acknowledged when the Tate opened a gallery here in 1993. St Ives was named by the *Guardian* newspaper as its seaside town of the year in 2007.

Newquay (right) has firmly established itself as Britain's surfing capital. Fistral beach (foreground) regularly stages major international surfing competitions. Each May Volkswagen and custom car drivers head to Newquay for the "Run to the Sun" music weekend.

Land's End (left) is the most westerly tip of England. Just over a mile (2km) offshore the Longships rocks have been guarded by a lighthouse since 1795.

BARNSTAPLE

In 2007 the new by-pass and elegant five-span bridge to the west of the busy town of Barnstaple (right) was completed, easing congestion in the town centre. Thought to be Britain's oldest borough, Barnstaple, on the banks of the river Taw, has been an important market town and trading centre since the Middle Ages. The Victorian cast-iron and glass Pannier Market houses Butchers Row, 10 shops dating from 1855.

LYNMOUTH

The Victorians called this part of Devon Little Switzerland. The town of Lynmouth (above), at the mouth of the Lyn, is surrounded by the hills of Exmoor. Thomas Gainsborough, who honeymooned here, declared it "the most delightful place for a landscape painter this country can boast".

SAUNTON SANDS

To the north of the estuary of the rivers Taw and Torridge, the beach at Saunton Sands (above) is three miles (5km) long. Behind it lies the UNESCO designated Biosphere Reserve of Braunton Burrows. This large area of dunes and marshes is home to a nature reserve, a golf course and a Ministry of Defence training ground.

WOOLACOMBE

The sandy beach at Woolacombe (left) is one of the best in the country. The sand stretches along Morte Bay for more than two miles (3.5km) between Baggy and Morte Points. Since the 1960s the village and beach have been popular with surfers, and in 2000 a surfing school opened here.

HURLSTONE POINT, PORLOCK

The rocky outcrop of Hurlstone Point (right) forms the eastern end of Porlock Bay and offers stunning views of the Bristol Channel. The mile-long shingle beach at Porlock is backed by salt marshes and the rolling hills of Exmoor. Out of season the area attracts a great variety of over-wintering birds.

ILFRACOMBE

The harbour at Ilfracombe (below) is the largest on the north Devon coast. It is separated from the Bristol Channel by Lantern Hill and protected by the larger Hillsborough Hill (foreground). Between March and October passenger ferries leave from the harbour bound for Lundy Island. Ilfracombe itself is a thriving, bustling holiday resort. The two conical white towers of the Landmark Theatre are a point of controversy for visitors and locals alike.

MINEHEAD

Overlooked by North Hill, Minehead (above) nestles between Exmoor and the sea. In the past there was a lantern in the parish church to guide travellers down from the moor and assist ships into harbour. A popular seaside resort, it has attracted holidaymakers since the mid-19th century. The white roofs (foreground) belong to the Skyline pavilion at the Butlins holiday resort, which opened in 1965.

The South-West Coast Path runs for 630 miles (1014km) from Minehead round the coast of Devon and Cornwall to Poole in Dorset. The West Somerset Railway, Britain's longest heritage railway, heads out in the other direction through unspoilt countryside skirting the Quantock Hills to Bishops Lydeard near Taunton.

CLIFTON SUSPENSION BRIDGE

When he was just 24, Isambard Kingdom Brunel was commissioned to build the Clifton Suspension Bridge (right). Its construction was dogged by financial and political problems and Brunel died in 1859 before it was finished. The bridge was finally completed in 1864 as a memorial to him. It spans the Avon Gorge 245ft (76m) above the river. Weight restrictions mean that only cars and light trucks can cross the bridge now, but nevertheless 4m vehicles use it every year.

BATH

The Romans were the first to document the UK's only natural hot springs at Bath (below). Taking the waters was a popular pastime for the wealthy in Elizabethan and Georgian times, when Bath experienced a building boom. The city has no fewer than eight Georgian crescents. Lansdown Crescent (below) was designed by John Palmer and built between 1789 and 1793. From the crescent high on Lansdown Hill there are extensive views over the city centre, including the famous Royal Crescent below.

Bath is now a World Heritage Site. The spa itself was closed for nearly 30 years but re-opened to the public in 2006 as the Thermae Bath Spa, with natural thermal baths and a rooftop pool.

LONGLEAT

Longleat House (below) is a fine example of high Elizabethan architecture. It was completed in 1580, and its beautiful parkland was landscaped in the 18th century by Capability Brown. It has remained in the same family and is the home of the Marquess of Bath. Longleat was the first stately home to open to the public, and the first safari park to open outside Africa.

GLASTONBURY TOR AND AVEBURY

The steep oval hill that is Glastonbury Tor (above) sits in the centre of Summerland Meadows, a plain forming part of the Somerset Levels. At the top of the hill is the roofless St Michael's Tower, the remains of a 15th-century church. There are many myths connected with Glastonbury, thought to be the birthplace of the legendary King Arthur.

Glastonbury is synonymous with the festival held at Worthy Farm six miles to the east of the tor. It is the world's biggest open-air music festival. In 2007 about 700 acts performed in front of 177,000 festival-goers who braved the rain and the mud.

The broad ditch and great stone circle of Avebury surround part of the village of Avebury (below). It predates Stonehenge (Avebury is about 5,000 years old), and is one of the largest and best Neolithic sites in Europe. The external ditch encloses about 28.5 acres. During excavations in the 1930s, stones that were found buried up to three feet below the surface were replaced in their original positions. The ancient monuments of Avebury and Stonehenge were together declared a World Heritage Site in 1986.

PART FOUR

CENTRAL ENGLAND

The geographical heart of Britain, central England is also the heart of the country's industrial base and prosperity. This is where the Industrial Revolution was born. By Victorian times the area known as the Black Country to the north and west of Birmingham was the most highly industrialised part of the country. It is a region of great contrasts. Its vibrant cities include Birmingham, Britain's second largest city, together with Derby, Leicester and Nottingham. To the south-west are the gentle hills and rural rolling landscapes of the Cotswolds, dotted with pretty villages and charming market towns. To complete the mix there are some of Britain's finest stately homes and imposing castles.

SPAGHETTI JUNCTION

It was not long before the Gravelly Hill Interchange (above) became universally known as Spaghetti Junction. This is junction six on the M6 motorway, where it meets the A38 (M) Aston Expressway and a host of other major and minor roads. It was Britain's first free-flow interchange without roundabouts or traffic lights. Construction started in 1968 and lasted for four years. The junction serves 18 routes and covers approximately 30 acres (12 ha). Five hundred and fifty-nine concrete columns up to 80ft (24.4m) high support the intricate road layout, which straddles three canals, two rivers and a main railway line.

COVENTRY

Leofric, Earl of Mercia and his wife Lady Godiva founded a Benedictine abbey at Coventry (right) in 1043. Angry at the heavy taxes her husband had imposed on the townspeople, Lady Godiva is reputed to have ridden naked through the town on horseback. The city's darkest hour came during the Second World War. On November 14 1940, a German air raid destroyed most of the historic city centre and St Michael's cathedral. You can still see the ruins of the old cathedral in the grounds of the new one, designed by Basil Spence. Benjamin Britten wrote his *War Requiem* for the opening of the new cathedral in 1962.

BIRMINGHAM BULLRING

The Bullring started life in 1166 when Birmingham (above) was first granted a charter giving it the right to hold its own market. The enclosed shopping centre that opened in 1964 was as big as 26 football pitches – one of the world's largest outside America. By the 1990s however it was widely disliked and considered a concrete monstrosity. It needed a facelift and, in 2000, a £450m refurbishment began. The result is an amazing glass-covered space with high quality shops. Most innovative is the new curvaceous Selfridges department store designed by Future Systems. The skin of this landmark building is covered by thousands of aluminium disks, making it look like the scales of a snake. The iconic circular Rotunda building survives from the 1960s, as does the historic St Martin's church, keeping watch over St Martin's Square at the heart of the complex.

WARWICK CASTLE

High above the river Avon perches Warwick Castle (above), one of England's great treasures. Ethelfleda, daughter of Alfred the Great, is said to have raised the first fortifications in 914AD. The earldom of Warwick is one of the oldest in England. The present shape of the castle, including Caesar's Tower and dungeon and the hexagonal Guy's Tower, dates from the 14th century. The State Rooms were extended a century later in honour of Elizabeth I, the first of several royal visitors. Today the castle is run commercially and attracts tens of thousands of visitors a year. There are jousting tournaments, falconry and even the world's biggest trebuchet, a siege machine that fires 33lb (15kg) stones.

BLENHEIM PALACE

John Churchill, the first Duke of Marlborough, received the Blenheim estate (left) from a grateful Queen Anne after his decisive victory over the French in 1704. She also paid for the building of the Baroque palace, designed by Sir John Vanburgh and built between 1705 and 1722. Forty years later the renowned garden designer Lancelot "Capability" Brown was given the task of landscaping the surrounding 2,100 acres of of parkland.

Winston Churchill, considered by many to be Britain's greatest prime minister, was born at Blenheim in 1874.

OXFORD

Oxford's High Street, known locally as The High, carves a broad swathe through Oxford from The Plain to Carfax Tower. This is the poet Matthew Arnold's "city of dreaming spires".

Either side of The High lie some of the university's 39 colleges and most important buildings. Behind the University Church of St Mary the Virgin sits the circular Radcliffe Camera, built in 1737 to house the Radcliffe Science Library. Today it is part of the adjacent Bodleian Library, one of the UK's five copyright deposit libraries.

Oxford is the oldest university in the English-speaking world. Teaching was underway in 1096 and 100 years later the first foreign student arrived. Today more than 130 nationalities are represented among the 18,000 student body.

GCHQ, CHELTENHAM

At the end of 2003, GCHQ (above) moved into its new home, popularly referred to as the Doughnut. GCHQ is the Government Communications Headquarters. It gathers intelligence for Britain's national security, and works closely with MI5 and MI6, the UK's intelligence agencies. It is a civil service department, reporting to the Foreign Office. The service was first set up in London after the First World War. Until 1946 it was known as the Government Code and Cypher School. In 1953 it moved to the outskirts of Cheltenham. For years GCHQ's existence was denied – official acknowledgement that it existed only came in 1983. The following year it was front-page news when Mrs Thatcher's government prohibited its employees from belonging to a trade union, declaring that this conflicted with national security. The ban was lifted in 1997.

IRONBRIDGE

One of the symbols of the Industrial Revolution, the cast-iron bridge (right) that spans the deep Severn Gorge in the heart of Shropshire was the world's first iron bridge. In the early 18th century the only way to cross the river was by ferry. But as industry developed in the region a more substantial crossing became necessary. In 1779 the Shrewsbury architect Thomas Farnolls Pritchard designed the Iron Bridge. It was 100ft (30m) long and constructed from 379 tons of iron, all cast at the nearby Coalbrookdale ironworks of Abraham Darby III. The village of Ironbridge grew up beside the bridge, and the steep hillside above the river is lined with 17th and 18th century workers' cottages. In 1986 the wider Ironbridge Gorge area was made a UNESCO World Heritage Site and it is now home to 10 diverse and fascinating museums.

GLOUCESTER CATHEDRAL

The Church of St Peter and the Holy and Indivisible Trinity (right) otherwise known as Gloucester Cathedral, is considered one of the seven most beautiful cathedrals in the world.

King Ethelred of Mercia granted land for the building of a church to a community of monks and nuns on the site here in 679. Four centuries later the foundation stone of the present building was laid. It took some 30 years to complete the Norman nucleus.

Today the cathedral has additions in a variety of Gothic styles. Its landmark central tower, built between 1450 and 1460, rises 225ft (68.5m) into the air.

Visitors can see a stained-glass window with images of golf dating from 1350, and a carving of people playing a medieval version of football. Harry Potter fans will know that the first two films were made here in 2000.

Every third year in August Gloucester Cathedral hosts the annual Three Choirs Festival. In other years, the festival passes in turn to Hereford and Worcester Cathedrals.

LEICESTER

One of the oldest cities in England, the history of Leicester (above) goes back nearly 2,000 years. The Romans founded it as *Ratae Coritanorum* in about 50AD, a military settlement on the Roman road known as Fosse Way. By the early 10th century it had become *Ligeraceaster*, "the town of the Ligor people". (Ligor was an early name for the river Soar, on which the city lies.) By the second half of the 20th century, Leicester had become one of the UK's most ethnically diverse cities, and today the Hindu celebrations for Diwali are the largest outside India.

Leicester City football club's home is Walkers Stadium, beside the river. Local boy Gary Lineker became a footballing legend and sports presenter and returned to open the new 32,500-seater bowl-shaped stadium in 2002.

The National Space Centre (left) is the UK's largest attraction dedicated to space. Work began on this project in 2000. When the iconic Rocket Tower was part finished, two rockets were installed and then the remaining sections of the hi-tech polythene walls were erected. The centre was opened by NASA astronaut Jeff Hoffman on June 30 2001.

DERBY

Derby (below) can trace its history back to Roman and Viking times. Some believe that the name Derby comes from the Danish *Deor-a-by* meaning "village of the deer", while others say it derives from its Roman name *Derventio*.

Bonnie Prince Charlie pitched camp at Derby in 1745 whilst on his way south to seize the English crown, staying at Exeter House and holding a council of war there.

The wheels of the Industrial Revolution were set in motion in Derby in the 18th century. In 1717 the town was the site of the first water-powered silk mill in Britain and in 1771 the first cotton-spinning mill was built by Sir Richard Arkwright at nearby Cromford, making the area a centre for cloth production. The town grew into a major railway centre, both as an important railway junction and as the home of major carriage and locomotive workshops and research based around the headquarters of the Midland Railway. Today Bombadier, Britain's only specialist train manufacturer, is still an important employer in Derby, as are Rolls-Royce and the Toyota Motor Corporation.

NOTTINGHAM

The history of Nottingham (left and above) is irrevocably linked with the legendary outlaw Robin Hood, who robbed the rich to give to the poor. He lived in Sherwood Forest, to the north of the city. His main rival was the Sheriff of Nottingham, a position that still exists, but which is today purely ceremonial.

At the heart of the town lies Old Market Square, the largest such square in England. It is dominated by the 200ft (61m) dome of the neo-Baroque Council House (centre right). The tower's bell, Little John, has the deepest tone of any bell in the country and on a clear day you can hear it seven miles (11km) away. Nottingham's two football clubs stand on opposite banks of the river Trent. Notts County FC, the oldest professional team in the world, play at the Meadow Lane ground on the north side, and to the south is the City Ground, the home of Nottingham Forest FC, who were once managed by Brian Clough. The famous Trent Bridge cricket ground, where Test match cricket has been played since 1899, lies south of the City Ground in West Bridgford.

LUTON AIRPORT

Thirty-two miles (51km) north of London, Luton Airport (above) is the fourth largest airport serving the London area. It opened in 1938 and during the Second World War served as the base for 264 Fighter Squadron. Civil use resumed in 1952 and the airport was developed for use by a number of holiday charter airlines. Today 15 airlines, including the low-cost carriers EasyJet and Ryanair, fly from London Luton to over 60 destinations.

DIANA ISLAND, ALTHORP

The Althorp estate has been the ancestral home of the Spencer family since the early 16th century. Althorp was the childhood home of Lady Diana Spencer who became the Princess of Wales on her marriage to Prince Charles in 1981. Amid national mourning after her untimely death in 1997, Diana's body was laid to rest on an island in the ornamental lake known as the Round Oval (right). A path of 36 oak trees, one for every year of her life, leads to the Round Oval. Each year the estate and house are are open to the public from July until September, apart from August 31, the anniversary of her death.

CLIVEDEN

The original hunting lodge, built by the 2nd Duke of Buckingham in 1666 to entertain his friends and mistress, was twice destroyed by fire. The classic Italianate house we now know as Cliveden (right) was built in 1851 by the architect Charles Barry. Owned by the National Trust, it sits in 376 acres of formal gardens and parkland.

In 1893 America's richest man, William Waldorf, bought Cliveden. (Apparently, Queen Victoria was not amused.) In the early 20th century it became the centre of high society and the Cliveden Set. By 1919 it was the home of Waldorf Astor and his wife Nancy, the first woman MP to take her seat in the House of Commons.

House guests at Cliveden included Charlie Chaplin and George Bernard Shaw, Winston Churchill and Theodore Roosevelt. In 1961 Cliveden was at the centre of the notorious Profumo Affair, which ended the career of the Minister for War, John Profumo. Today this glorious house is run as a luxury hotel.

PART FIVE

EASTERN ENGLAND

From the mouth of the Thames north to the waters of the Wash and the river Humber, eastern England encompasses the ancient kingdom of East Anglia and the modern county of Lincolnshire. Eastern England has two unique areas of countryside – the Fens and the Norfolk Broads. The coast is blessed with long sand and shingle beaches, fringed by mudflats, saltmarsh and reedbeds, all havens for a remarkable range of wildlife. The coastal areas of North Norfolk and Suffolk contain some of the finest seaside resorts in England. Inland the magnificent cities of Cambridge, Ely, Norwich and Lincoln have a fine heritage of cathedral architecture and splendid ancient buildings. On the coast are the thriving ports of Harwich, Felixstowe, Immingham and Grimsby.

THE ESSEX MARSHES

The coastline between the rivers Crouch and Colne is one of Britain's most important areas for wildlife. As the tide recedes, the low-lying mudflats and salt marshes reveal themselves in intricate patterns (above).

The national nature reserve on the north bank of the Blackwater estuary is home to bearded tits and other species that breed and over-winter here. It is also an important feeding ground for Brent geese, cormorants, plovers and oystercatchers.

The area is also popular with the sailing fraternity. The Burnham Week yacht regatta has been held every August at Burnham-on-Crouch for over a hundred years.

SOUTHEND-ON-SEA

With the advent of the railway, Southend (right) became a popular seaside resort for Londoners. Its iconic pier has survived a number of fires (the last in 2005) as well as the occasional ship crashing into it. At 1.34 miles (2.15km) it is the world's longest pleasure pier, opened in stages between 1889 and 1929. In its heyday in 1949 it attracted 7m visitors.

MALDON

Salt has been important to Maldon (above) for centuries. The Domesday book of 1086 lists a population of 180 and 45 saltpans in the area. A Guild of Saltmakers was founded in 1394; the Maldon Crystal Sea Salt company, founded in 1882, still thrives as a family company. The English culinary guru Delia Smith includes Maldon salt in her list of every cook's "must haves".

Maldon got its name from *mael*, meaning meeting place and *dun*, meaning hill, in Saxon times. The town stands at the head of the Blackwater estuary, its attractive waterfront dotted with fine examples of restored Thames sailing barges.

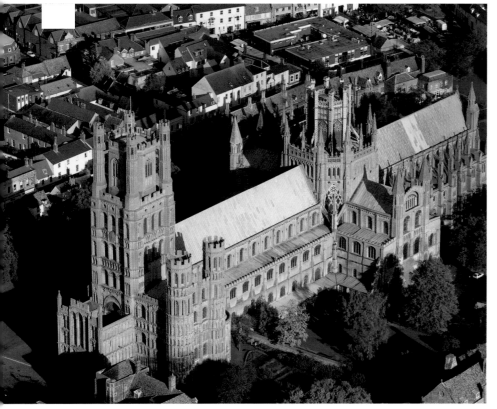

THE GREAT CATHEDRAL CITIES

The great cathedrals of eastern England have been symbols of the Christian faith since the 11th and 12th centuries.

Norwich cathedral (above) is famed for its unique two-storey cloisters and its 315ft (96m) tower, the second tallest in England. It is one of just three cathedrals in England without any bells; the others are the superb Romanesque Ely cathedral (left) and Salisbury in Wiltshire. Ely cathedral is known locally as "the ship of the Fens" because of its slender tower which looms above the surrounding flat countryside.

The 13th century painted wooden ceiling of Peterborough cathedral (right) is the only one in Britain, and one of only four in Europe.

Lincoln cathedral (far right) is Britain's third largest and it has the tallest medieval tower in Europe.

CAMBRIDGE

When students fled from the hostile townsfolk of Oxford in 1209, they set up an alternative seat of learning in Cambridge. This makes it the second oldest university in Britain.

Peterhouse, dating from 1284, is the oldest Cambridge college. Women students were only admitted as full members of the university in 1948, and there are still three women-only colleges: Newnham, New Hall and Lucy Cavendish.

The foundation stone of the King's College chapel (left) was laid by King Henry VI in 1446, but the impressive building was only completed 69 years later. Today King's College choir delights millions of listeners worldwide on Christmas Eve in the traditional Festival of Nine Lessons and Carols, first broadcast in 1928.

IPSWICH

Ipswich (above), on the river Orwell, is one of England's oldest towns. In Anglo-Saxon times it was the main centre between London and York for trade with Scandinavia.

The town has had a remarkable crop of residents: Henry VIII's closest ally, Cardinal Wolsey, the painters John Constable and Thomas Gainsborough, and Admiral Nelson. More recently Alf Ramsey managed Ipswich Town football team for eight years from 1955. As manager of the national team he helped England win the World Cup in 1966. South of Ipswich the Orwell Bridge (left) carries 60,000 vehicles across the river on the A14 every day.

SIZEWELL

Sizewell (above) on the Suffolk coast is dominated by its two nuclear power stations. Sizewell A (right of picture) was closed at the end of 2006: the decommissioning process will last about 100 years and is forecast to cost an estimated £1.2bn. The white dome at Sizewell B, Britain's only large pressurised water nuclear reactor, houses the outer of the reactor's two containment buildings. Sizewell B produces three per cent of the country's energy needs.

FELIXSTOWE DOCKS

Britain's largest container port, Felixstowe (left) is the fourth largest in Europe after Rotterdam, Hamburg and Antwerp. It is also an attractive seaside resort and is well-known for the extensive and glorious gardens that run the length of the promenade and into the town centre. On the seafront is the Spa Pavilion Theatre, which features ballet, drama and pantomime as well as a modern cinema. At Felixstowe Ferry, part of the old town, there is a ferry across the estuary to Bawdsey.

SEALS, WIND FARMS AND BEACHES

Preferring sandbanks and gently sloping sandy beaches, several colonies of grey and common seals have made their home along the Norfolk coast. At Blakeney Point to the north (left) the colony numbers about 500, regularly observed by tourists on boat trips from Blakeney harbour. The National Trust acquired the area around Blakeney Point in 1912 and set up the first nature reserve in Norfolk. The Scroby Sands wind farm (left) is located one and a half miles (2.5km) off the coast of Great Yarmouth. Thirty wind turbines make up Britain's first commercial offshore facility, which cost £75m when it was commissioned in 2004. The wind farm can generate enough energy for 30,000 homes; this could mean 68,000 tonnes less carbon dioxide and 600 tonnes less sulphur dioxide emitted into the atmosphere every year.

The east Norfolk coast boasts some exceptional unspoilt sandy beaches. The dunes between the sea and the village of Winterton-on-Sea (below) are home to a flock of terns and a rare colony of natterjack toads. Here in 2002 the southern emerald damselfly was first spotted in Britain.

KING'S LYNN AND THE WASH

The town of Bishop's Lynn was named after Bishop Herbert de Losinga but after the Dissolution of the Monasteries in 1538 it was renamed King's Lynn (left). It is on the banks of the Great Ouse river, close to where it flows into the Wash and the North Sea. Norfolk meets Lincolnshire at the Wash, where four rivers flow into one of Britain's largest estuaries. The square-shaped Wash and the surrounding low-lying Fens are a wildlife special protection site under EU legislation.

THE BROADS

The Norfolk Broads were formed by flooding of old peat beds. Since the early 20th century boating on the lock-free waterways has been a popular holiday pastime. Heigham Sound (below) flows into Hickling Broad, the largest broad and one of the biggest stretches of water in East Anglia. Barton Turf (below left), on Barton Broad, is a haven for visitors – as shown by the large number of boats moored at the village's staithe, or landing stage.

BOSTON

Some say Boston (above) began life as "St Botolph's town". It stands on the once tidal river Haven. By the 13th century Boston was an important centre for trade with Europe, and the most important commodity was wool. Salt was also an important export, which was produced all along the coastlines of Lincolnshire and Norfolk.

In 1607 a group of Nottinghamshire pilgrims attempted to set sail from Boston to escape the rigorous teachings of the church. This emigration was deemed illegal but the following year they succeeded, and settled in Leiden in the Netherlands. In 1620 several of those same pilgrims sailed to New England aboard the *Mayflower*. They established the city of Boston, Massachusetts, 10 years later.

Today St Botolph's Church takes pride of place in the town. It is locally called the Stump: its tower is 272.5ft (83m) tall and is England's tallest parish church without a spire.

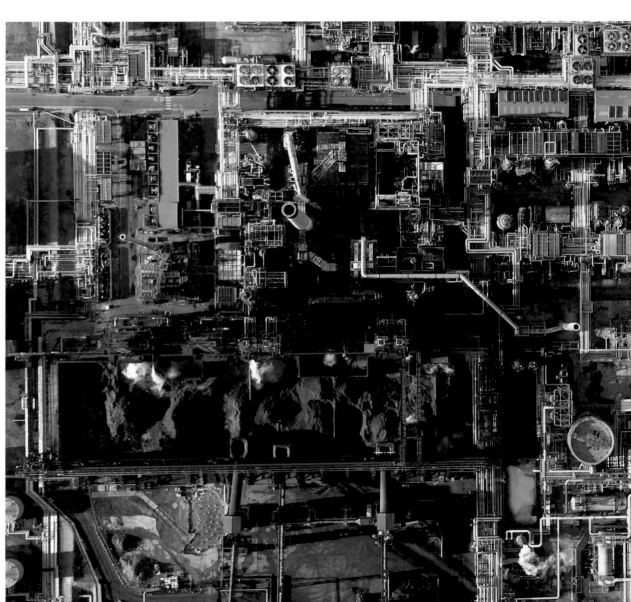

GRIMSBY

Legend has it that Grimsby (left), on the Humber estuary, was founded in the 9th century by a Danish fisherman called Grim. Its location provided shelter for boats.

Over the centuries the town grew into an important trading and fishing port. Six years after the Grimsby Docks Act of 1845 the 309ft (94m) high Dock Tower at the entrance to Royal Dock was completed.

With the arrival of refrigeration 100 years later Grimsby was the busiest and largest fishing port in the world. It was here that Birds Eye produced the first fish finger in 1955. Grimsby, together with nearby Immingham, is the UK's largest port in terms of tonnage and in 2006 handled some 57 million tonnes.

IMMINGHAM DOCKS

George V opened Immingham docks (above) in 1913. They are the country's largest deep-sea docks and, with the surrounding industrial facilities, handle large volumes of coal and iron ore, pulp and paper, oil and petro-chemicals from all over the world. There are two refineries (left) at Killingholme, to the west of the docks.

PART SIX

YORKSHIRE

England's largest county boasts a diverse landscape which few areas of Britain can match, from the mighty cities of west and south Yorkshire, and the rural charms of the moors and dales to its stunning coastline. The urban regions have a long history of mining and manufacturing and many of the area's landmarks still reflect this industrial past. North Yorkshire has two areas of outstanding natural beauty – the North York Moors and the Yorkshire Dales. The Yorkshire coastline is one of the county's crowning glories. Between the Heritage Coast in the north and Spurn Head in the south are a succession of dramatic bays, glorious beaches and cliffs dotted with pretty fishing villages and historic seaside resorts such as Whitby and Scarborough.

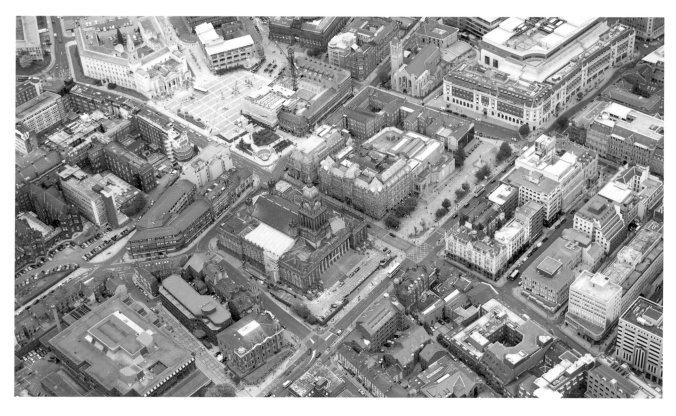

LEEDS

From the Middle Ages, Leeds (above) was an important manufacturer of woollen cloth. The arrival of canal and rail transport transformed the city into an industrial giant and today it is the most important and vibrant city in Yorkshire. At its heart is the imposing Town Hall, opened by Queen Victoria in 1858. It contrasts with the 1930s Civic Hall, in Millennium Square, built in white Portland stone, which houses the city council. Today Leeds offers a varied cultural programme including an annual German Christmas Market, a summer *Mela*, a West Indian carnival and the world-famous Leeds International Piano Competition, held every three years.

BRADFORD

In Norman times the original village of Bradford (right) sprang up around the "broad ford" over the river now called the Bradford Beck. Since the 13th century textiles have been an important local industry, but the Industrial Revolution saw Bradford become world-famous for worsted cloth. The city thrived and developed an innovative manufacturing base. This innovation continues today, but the "dark satanic mills" have been replaced by high-tech, leisure, financial and service industries. In addition to the Leisure Exchange complex (foreground), Bradford also boasts the National Media Museum, one of the most visited museums outside London.

HAWORTH

Set amid the bleak Pennine Moors above the Worth Valley, Haworth (above) is inextricably linked with the Brontë name. The Reverend Patrick Brontë and his young family arrived in 1820 when he became the local vicar. The parsonage remained the family home for the rest of their lives and it was here that the sisters wrote their most famous novels: Charlotte's *Jane Eyre*, Emily's *Wuthering Heights* and Anne's *Agnes Grey* all appearing in 1847. The parsonage is now home to the Brontë Parsonage Museum and the Brontë Society. Another local attraction running through the village is the Keighley and Worth Valley Railway. Opened in 1867 by local mill-owners, the line was closed in 1962 by British Rail but just six years later enthusiastic volunteers opened it up again. With trains hauled by steam engines, the line is popular with makers of period films, such as *The Railway Children*.

RICHMOND

Situated on the banks of the river Swale, Richmond (left) was founded in 1071 by the Norman Alan Rufus on land granted to him by William the Conqueror. The town grew up around the castle built on the *riche-mont* (strong hill) from which its name derives. The castle's original French keep was replaced in the 12th century by a 100-foot high keep, with 11-foot thick walls, which still stands today. The Green Bridge across the river Swale (foreground) is so-called because it leads over to Richmond Green.

HAREWOOD HOUSE

This magnificent country house (below left), the home of Earl and Countess Lascelles, was built by the York architect John Carr between 1759 and 1772 on the instructions of Edwin Lascelles whose father had made his fortune in the ribbon trade, from his position as collector of customs in Barbados and his directorship of the East India Company. The interiors were the work of Robert Adam and much of the furniture is by Thomas Chippendale. In the 1840s the south façade of the house was remodelled by Sir Charles Barry, the architect of the Houses of Parliament. The grounds were laid out by Lancelot "Capability" Brown. To the south of the house is an ornamental garden with intricate flower-beds, fountains and herbaceous borders. Still the home of the Lascelles family, Harewood won a "large visitor attraction of the year award" in 2003, and is home to the Yorkshire Planetarium.

ASKRIGG

In Norse, Askrigg meant "the ridge where ash trees grew". This attractive village in Wensleydale (left) can trace its history back to the Iron Age. In 1587 Elizabeth I granted a charter for a weekly market every Thursday and Askrigg flourished as a thriving market town. Today, television viewers will recognise it as the fictional Darrowby, the setting for the BBC TV series *All Creatures Great and Small*.

MIDDLEHAM CASTLE

The ruins of the castle dominate Middleham (below) in Wensleydale. The keep, one of the largest in England, and the original bailey date from the 12th century. The castle is where Richard III grew up, his son Edward was born and died aged 11 and his wife Anne died just a year later in 1485. He was killed the same year at the Battle of Bosworth. In 1646, during the Civil War, Parliament ordered the eastern part of the castle to be destroyed. The surrounding area is a centre for the training of racehorses.

BOLTON ABBEY

Bolton Abbey (left) on the banks of the river Wharfe, was founded by the Augustinian order in 1151. The abbey prospered until the Dissolution of the Monasteries in 1539 when it was reduced in size and became the Priory Church of St Mary and St Cuthbert. The east end remains in ruins. In the 19th century, major improvements were carried out to the church under the guidance of the Devonshire family on whose land the abbey stands. These included the installation of windows by the famous architect August Pugin. Close by is Barden Tower, the old hunting lodge and home of the Earls of Skipton.

69

SHEFFIELD

From modest beginnings, Sheffield (below) developed into a market town in the 13th century. By 1600 it had become the principal centre in England for the production of cutlery. Crucible steel was invented here in the 1740s, as was Sheffield plate, imitation silver plate made from copper sheet rolled between thin silver sheets.

Surrounded by seven hills, Sheffield has 50 parks and five river valleys. It is remarkably green – one third of the metropolitan area lies within the Peak District National Park and the city has many sites of special scientific interest. Recently the city has re-positioned itself as a sporting and technology centre. The 25,000-seater Don Valley Stadium, built for the 1991 World Student Games, is the largest athletics stadium in the UK.

ROTHERHAM

Rotherham (right) grew up on the eastern bank of the river Don where a low rise gave a commanding position for All Saints parish church, now Rotherham Minster. Its golden age came with the arrival of coal, iron and later steel. The River Don Navigation Canal was built to support these new industries.

In 1854 Samuel Beal & Co, a local firm, produced the cast-iron armour-plating for Brunel's steamship the *SS Great Britain*.

The town centre was largely redeveloped during the 20th century but the 15th century Chapel of our Lady of Rotherham on the medieval Chantry Bridge survives. One of only four remaining bridge chapels in the country, travellers could give thanks for their safe arrival in the town or pray for a safe journey on departure.

DONCASTER

Since Roman times, when it was called *Danum*, Doncaster (above) has been a major junction and has developed into an important trading centre. In the 16th century the town became known for horse-breeding and subsequently horse-racing. Doncaster racecourse is one of the oldest and largest in the country. This is where the world's oldest classic horse race, the St Leger Stakes, was first held in 1776 and is still run today.

The railways came to the town in the 1850s, with Doncaster workshops producing such famous steam engines as the *Mallard* and the *Flying Scotsman*. Today Doncaster station is served by the largest number of train operators in the UK.

CONISBROUGH CASTLE

The small town of Conisbrough (right) lies roughly midway between Doncaster and Rotherham on the river Don. The imposing castle was probably built in the 12th century by Henry II's half-brother Hamelin de Warenne, on the site of an earlier Norman castle. The 100-foot high circular keep is supported by six wedge-shaped buttresses and dominates the ruins. Restoration of the castle began in 1992; the floors of the castle have been reinstated and the conical roof is once more in place. The fame of Conisbrough Castle rests largely on the fact that it was the setting for Sir Walter Scott's novel *Ivanhoe*.

HARROGATE

In 1571 William Slingsby discovered that the water from the Tewitt Well had medicinal properties. By the 19th and early 20th centuries Harrogate had developed into an elegant spa town to rival Bath and Buxton in the Peak District. It attracted the English elite and European nobility; the British royal family were regular visitors to the town. By the time of the First World War the spa was in decline and during the Second World War Harrogate's many hotels were filled with government offices evacuated from London. This helped create Harrogate's reputation as a conference and exhibition centre. Today the town is also famous for hosting political party conferences.

CASTLE HOWARD

Castle Howard (left) is one of the grandest private houses in Britain. It has been home to the Howard family for over 300 years. The first phase of the house was built in Baroque style in the early 18th century by Sir John Vanburgh and Nicholas Hawksmoor for the third Earl of Carlisle. Around 1715 the Earl switched his attention to the design of the gardens and grounds. The west wing was completed a century later in contrasting Palladian style. In the 1,000 acres of beautiful gardens and grounds lie Vanburgh's Temple of the Four Winds and (foreground) the Castle Howard Mausoleum, designed by Hawksmoor. This is still the private burial place of the Howard family.

When Castle Howard featured in the popular television adaptation of Evelyn Waugh's novel *Brideshead Revisited* in 1981 the house became a star in its own right.

WETHERBY

Dramatically sited on the steep banks of the river Wharfe, Wetherby (right) is presided over by the parish church of St James. The magnificent bridge which spans the river is a scheduled ancient monument. The town is exactly 198 miles (318km) from both London and Edinburgh and for hundreds of years it has been a major crossroads. It was an important staging point on the Great North Road, with nearly 40 public houses and inns catering for stagecoach travellers.

Wetherby can trace its history back to the Domesday Book. In 1240 it was granted a royal charter to hold markets in the town square, a tradition which is upheld every Thursday. The town's peaceful appearance today contrasts with some violent history – in 1314 it was burned by the Scots after the Battle of Bannockburn and in 1461 nearby Towton was the scene of one of the bloodiest battles in the Wars of the Roses.

YORK MINSTER

The largest Gothic cathedral in northern Europe, York Minster (left) soars above the city. Although there was a Christian presence since the 4th century, the first church on the site is thought to have been built in haste in 627 for the baptism of Edwin, King of Northumbria.

In the 13th century Archbishop Walter de Gray wanted a building to rival Canterbury cathedral. Building began in 1220 but it took 250 years to complete. The new cathedral was consecrated in 1472. The Minster is 485ft (148m) in length and each of the three towers is 196ft (60m) high. The choir is the second highest in England, surpassed only by that of Westminster Abbey.

The Minster's stained-glass is remarkable: its Great East Window soars to 76ft (23.7m) and is the world's largest example of medieval stained-glass, while the famous Rose Window in the south transept celebrates the end of the Wars of the Roses and the marriage of Henry VII to Elizabeth of York, uniting the royal houses of York and Lancaster. In November 2005 Dr John Sentamu was enthroned as the 97th Archbishop of York, the second most senior clergyman in the Church of England, to the accompaniment of African drums during the service.

THIRSK

The small market town of Thirsk (right) has grown up around a large medieval square where open-air markets are still held every Monday and Saturday. It lies in the Vale of Mowbray, close to the North York Moors National Park. The Domesday Book in 1089 refers to it as *Tresche*, the Old Norse name meaning "marshy place".

Today Thirsk attracts visitors to the home of local vet Alf Wight. Under the pen name James Herriot he wrote about his experiences as a young vet in Thirsk and Sowerby after the war. His book *All Creatures Great and Small*, first published in 1972, was a publishing sensation and later a popular television series. The Georgian house in which he lived and practised at 23 Kirkgate is now a museum; the cluttered 1950s interiors in which he worked have been lovingly recreated.

NEWBY HALL

Sir Christopher Wren guided the design of Newby Hall (below) built in 1697. Since 1748 it has been home to the Compton family, whose ancestor William Weddell bought the property and enlarged it during the 1760s. The interior was remodelled by a variety of architects, including Robert Adam, and it is an exceptional example of 18th century interior design.

The present grounds were laid out in the 1920s, with herbaceous borders and a dramatic broad grass walk leading down to the river Ure. In 2007 Newby Hall was used for the filming of the television adaptation of Jane Austen's novel *Mansfield Park*. Still privately owned, the house and gardens are open to the public from March to September.

NORTHALLERTON

Saxon in origin, Northallerton (above) lies in the centre of the Vale of York. It became a town in 1200 when it was granted its first royal charter. Over the centuries it developed into the area's market town and an important stop on the north-south route. At the height of the coaching age, Northallerton boasted four coaching inns along its fine curving High Street, serving both passengers and horses on their journeys north to Scotland and south to London. When the railway arrived in 1841 the town's importance as a centre of communications was assured. The line from London to Edinburgh passed through, as did the line linking the West Riding with the east coast port of Middlesbrough. Northallerton is a busy centre for light industry and agriculture and has a regular livestock mart. On Wednesdays and Saturdays the High Street comes alive at the weekly markets when stalls line both sides of the street right up to the steps of the Town Hall.

KILBURN WHITE HORSE

The largest of Britain's 11 white horses, the Kilburn White Horse (right) is cut into the hillside of Sutton Bank on the edge of the North York Moors, above the village of Kilburn. It was created in 1857 at the instigation of Thomas Taylor, a local resident, who was inspired by the white horse carved out of the Downs at Uffington in Oxfordshire. It took 33 men to cut the horse out of the hillside and six tonnes of lime were used to whiten the exposed rock. The white horse faces south-west and is clearly visible from many miles away, particularly from the east coast main railway line south of Thirsk. During the Second World War, the white horse was covered over to prevent enemy bombers from using it as a navigation point.

HELMSLEY

The strong barbican entrances and unusual D-shaped east tower of Helmsley Castle still dominate the town (below) to this day. The first castle was built by a soldier named Walter Espec (nicknamed Walter the Woodpecker) in 1120 and he surrounded it with spectacular banks and ditches. About 60 years later the castle was strengthened and rebuilt in stone by a Crusader, Robert de Roos. In 1644, during the Civil War, the Royalist occupants of the castle were starved into submission by the Parliamentarians under Sir Thomas Fairfax. Fairfax then ordered the castle defences to be dismantled and gave the mansion to his daughter. Today Helmsley is one of the most attractive towns in North Yorkshire. Located on the Thirsk to Scarborough road, it is an ideal centre for touring and its centre is full of pubs, gift shops and galleries. The prize possession of All Saints' church, situated just off the main square, is a letter written by the explorer David Livingstone when he was in Africa.

PICKERING

The busy and elegant market town of Pickering (above) is located on the southern edge of the North York Moors. Today it is a thriving market town and popular tourist destination with its imposing Norman motte and bailey castle, built by William the Conqueror. The town lies at the southern end of the North Yorkshire Moors Railway. A casualty of the Beeching cuts in 1965, the 18-mile long line between Pickering and Grosmont was re-opened in 1973 as the UK's second longest heritage line, with many of the trains steam-hauled. Due to the unspoilt nature of the scenery along the line, the railway has featured in several major films including JK Rowling's *Harry Potter and the Philosopher's Stone.* In the town centre, the Beck Isle Museum of Rural Life gives an insight into farming life through the centuries.

RIEVAULX ABBEY

Twelve monks from Clairvaux Abbey in France set out to colonise the north of England and Scotland. In 1132, when they reached this secluded wooded valley by the river Rye, they founded Rievaulx Abbey (right). Over the years the abbey grew to become one of the most important Cistercian houses in Yorkshire, second only to Fountains Abbey. Its profitable businesses – mining lead and iron, rearing sheep and selling wool to buyers from all over Europe – enabled Rievaulx to amass great wealth, and at its peak there were some 140 monks in residence. The monastic community was already on the wane when Henry VIII issued the decree of the Dissolution of the Monasteries across England. Rievaulx was rendered uninhabitable in 1538 and stripped of all valuable materials. Today the impressive ruins are looked after by English Heritage.

HUMBER BRIDGE

There have been numerous plans to span the Humber estuary: in 1872 a tunnel was proposed; in 1928 a multi-span truss bridge, and in 1959 a suspension bridge finally received approval. Construction began in 1973 and on completion in 1981 the 7282ft (2,220m) bridge was the longest single-span suspension bridge in the world. Today the Humber Bridge (right) is the world's fourth longest and more than 100,000 vehicles use it every week.

SCARBOROUGH

"Are you going to Scarborough Fair?" asks the song. For 500 years this was a huge event: every year until the 18th century, merchants from all over Europe traded here for six weeks between Assumption and Michaelmas Day. The town (below) was founded in 966 by the Viking raider Thorgils Skarthi. In 1626 Mrs Elizabeth Farrow found that the waters from a nearby stream had medicinal properties. She set off a chain reaction and people flocked to Scarborough Spa, Britain's first seaside resort. Anne Brontë, who had been suffering from consumption, visited with her sister Charlotte in the hope that the sea air would cure her. Sadly she died at the age of 28 and is buried in St Mary's churchyard. With its busier South Bay separated from the more tranquil North Bay by the Castle Headland, Scarborough has developed into the largest holiday resort on the Yorkshire coast.

FLAMBOROUGH HEAD

The chalk headland of Flamborough Head (right) juts some seven miles (11.3km) into the North Sea and is one of the most prominent features on England's east coast. Today Flamborough is one of the largest RSPB reserves in the country; over 250,000 seabirds nest here annually. The best time to see the birds is during the nesting season from June to September. The visitor centre is open throughout the year.

Two lighthouses attest to the danger to shipping that the headland poses. The 85ft (26m) high Flamborough lighthouse was built in 1806 without the use of scaffolding. Further back is the old Beacon light tower which dates from around 1674. Perched almost on the very edge of the 400ft (122m) cliffs is the more modern foghorn station (foreground).

STAITHES

Once the largest fishing port on the north-east coast of England, the picturesque village of Staithes (above) – pronounced "Steers" by the locals – is today a popular tourist destination. It is sheltered by the lofty outcrop of Cow Bar Nab across Roxby Beck.

At the turn of the 20th century there were 80 full-time fishing boats putting out to sea from the harbour. Today there is just one – a traditional, locally-made vessel known as a *coble*.

Staithes' most famous resident was the great explorer and navigator James Cook. As a young man he worked as a grocer's apprentice in the village in 1745-1746, before moving to Whitby. From there he embarked on his illustrious naval career, undertaking voyages to Australia, New Zealand and the Pacific.

PART SEVEN

NORTH-WEST ENGLAND

Generations of writers and poets, painters and musicians have found inspiration amid the spectacular scenery in the north-west of England. It ranges from Cheshire and the medieval walled city of Chester, to Lancashire, Cumbria and the dramatic beauty of the Lake District. In the cities, the grime of the Victorian industrial era has been transformed. Today visitors come for the rich history and 21st-century design of Liverpool, European Capital of Culture in 2008, and Manchester with its sophisticated shopping, sport and nightlife.

SALFORD QUAYS

The cultural centre of Salford Quays sits on the site of the old Salford Docks on the Manchester Ship Canal. The docks closed in 1982 after a drastic slump in shipping hit the area hard. Millions of pounds have been spent on regeneration: in 2000 The Lowry Theatre and Art Gallery opened, named after the Salford artist LS Lowry, famous for his paintings of matchstick men in industrial settings. Across the water sits the shining Imperial War Museum North. Daniel Libeskind designed the building as a globe broken into three fragments, representing the devastating effects of war on the world. Linking the two is the Millennium lifting footbridge, which was the finishing line in the marathon during the 2002 Manchester Commonwealth Games.

BEETHAM TOWER, MANCHESTER

The tallest building in the UK outside London, the Beetham Tower
is 554ft (169m) high. It takes its name from its developers, the
Beetham Organization, and stands on Deansgate, Manchester's two-
mile long main thoroughfare. Locals call it the Hilton Tower, as the
first 23 of its 48 floors house a Hilton hotel. The remaining floors
are apartments – with the top two-storey penthouse enjoying
spectacular views, as far as Snowdonia on a clear day.

MANCHESTER STUDIOS

The television studios on Manchester's Quay Street were formerly
known as Granada TV Studios. They are now owned by 3sixtymedia.
They are still used for the filming of the UK's longest running
television soap opera, *Coronation Street*. Corrie, as it is affectionately
nicknamed, was first broadcast in December 1960. Between 1988 and
1999 fans flocked to the studios to visit the set and walk down the
famous street, with its buildings built of reclaimed Salford brick.
Weatherfield, the fictional suburb of Manchester where *Coronation
Street* is based, was loosely based on Salford. From the original cast,
such characters as Ena Sharples, Annie Walker and Elsie Tanner
have come and gone, but the character of Ken Barlow lives on.
He is still played by the same actor, William Roache.

LIVERPOOL WATERSIDE

Three buildings take pride of place at Pier Head. They are often referred to as Liverpool's Three Graces. The two largest clock-faces in Britain top the Liver Building's twin towers, built in 1911. It is still the head office of the Royal Liver Friendly Society. Next door is the Cunard Building, constructed between 1914 and 1917. It is irregular in shape – 30ft wider on the landside than on the waterside.

Completing the trio is the Port of Liverpool Building, dating from 1907. Ferries still cross the river Mersey to Birkenhead, and now there are also two road tunnels under the river.

The vibrant city of Liverpool is continually re-inventing itself. Much of the dock area and the city centre is in the process of regeneration. Liverpool has been designated European Capital of Culture 2008.

LIVERPOOL'S CATHEDRALS

Liverpool is a city rich in religious buildings: two cathedrals, a Greek Orthodox church, a Swedish seamen's church, synagogues, mosques, Hindu temples and a Sikh *gurdwara*. The poet John Betjeman considered the Anglican cathedral (top right) designed by Sir Giles Gilbert Scott one of the 20th century's great buildings. Begun in 1904 but only completed in 1978, it is full of superlatives: the world's longest nave, the tallest Gothic arches, the highest and heaviest peal of bells. Facing it, at the other end of Hope Street, stands Sir Frederick Gibberd's circular Catholic Metropolitan Cathedral of Christ the King (bottom right), consecrated in 1967. Its nickname, Paddy's Wigwam, is a recognition of the Irish connection of many in its congregation. Although the cathedrals hail from different periods, both buildings are much loved locally.

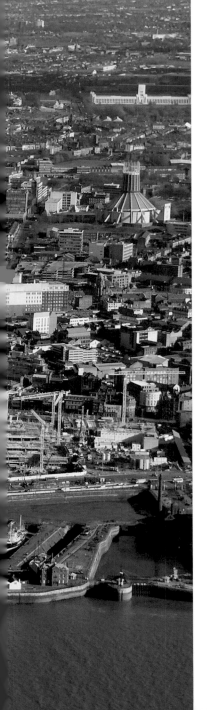

BLACKPOOL

Still the UK's most popular seaside resort, Blackpool is said to have got its name from the black pool of water that flowed from a peat bog into the Irish Sea at this point. It first became known as a tourist resort in the 19th century. In its heyday, between 1900-1950, the beaches and promenade were crowded with factory workers from the north on their annual holiday. It is still the most popular holiday destination for Glaswegians. Today, Blackpool boasts more hotel and guesthouse beds than the whole of Portugal.

Blackpool's famous tower was inspired by the Eiffel Tower. Constructed between 1897-1898, it stands 518ft (158m) high, and served as a radar station in the Second World War. It dominates the skyline and at its foot are bars, restaurants, the famous Tower Ballroom and Tower Circus. Close by, at the Winter Gardens, is the Opera House, one of Europe's biggest theatres. With miles of beaches and donkey rides during the summer months, Blackpool's attraction is timeless. One of the best ways to enjoy the extensive seaside promenade is to ride aboard the legendary trams which travel the 11-mile (18km) route between Starr Gate and Fleetwood. From August to November every year the bright light displays known as the Illuminations stretch along the seven miles (11km) of Blackpool's seafront.

PLEASURE BEACH

Close to South Pier, one of three in the town, is Blackpool's Pleasure Beach (right), offering thrills and spills – but not for the faint-hearted! There are over 125 rides including the Grand National, Europe's first twin-track racing coaster, and the blue-painted Pepsi Max Big One, which is 235ft (72m) high, and can reach speeds of 87mph (140kph).

LANCASTER

Bounded by the river Lune, from where it takes its name, and traversed by the Lancaster Canal (right), the city of Lancaster can trace its history back to Roman times. It was granted its first charter as a market town in 1193 and finally achieved city status in 1937.

Roger de Pitou founded the castle (below) at the end of the 11th century. Part of the Norman keep still survives today. Since 1196 the castle has been a prison and only certain parts are open to the public. In 1612, the notorious Pendle witch trial here led to the hanging of 10 people for witchcraft. More people were hanged by the court here than any other town in England.

The Priory Church of St Mary stands close to the castle. This beautiful 15th century building is largely medieval, although the original priory dates back to 1094. Close by is the Roman Catholic Lancaster cathedral, also known as St Peter, which overlooks Lancaster Canal.

Lancaster station is one of the main railway stations on the west coast mainline between London Euston and Glasgow. It used to be called Lancaster Castle station to distinguish it from the other station, now closed. Re-modelled in 1902, the new buildings were given a mock-Elizabethan look to mirror the style of the nearby castle.

VALE OF LUNE

The river Lune meanders some 44 miles (71km) between Wath in Cumbria and the Irish Sea at Plover Scar, near Lancaster. Just outside Lancaster it is crossed by a number of bridges including the Lune Millennium Bridge for cyclists and pedestrians. The 131ft (40m) Y-shaped vertical support for the bridge echoes the city's maritime history.

MORECAMBE BAY

The largest area of intertidal mudflats and sand in the UK, Morecambe Bay covers an area of 120 square miles. There have been royally appointed Queen's sandpilots for centuries to help people cross the treacherous sands safely. About £6m worth of cockles are collected here every year, but unwary pickers can find themselves caught by the fast-rising tides.

The resort of Morecambe has attracted many visitors over the years. The town's most famous son, Eric Morecambe, was one half of the Morecambe and Wise comedy duo.

CONISTON AND CONISTON WATER

Set back from the water's edge, the pretty village of Coniston (above) sits at the foot of The Old Man of Coniston, at 2635ft (803m) one of the highest points in the Furness Fells. The Victorian poet, author and artist John Ruskin lived across the lake in Brantwood and claimed that the view towards The Old Man of Coniston was "the best in all of England".

   Coniston Water (right) is the third largest stretch of water in the Lake District, after Windermere and Ullswater. Here in 1939 Sir Malcolm Campbell set a world water speed record of 141.74mph (228.108kph) in his boat *Bluebird K4*. His son Donald tragically died on the lake in 1967 while attempting to exceed a speed of 300mph (483kph) in *Bluebird K7*. The name Bluebird lives on as the name of a beer brewed by the local Coniston Brewery.

ARNSIDE

The railway line along the Cumbrian coast is one of the most scenic in Britain. The 50 arches of the Arnside Viaduct take the Furness Line between Barrow-in- Furness and Carnforth. It stretches over the estuary of the river Kent, where it enters Morecambe Bay. The village of

Arnside appears to emerge from the thickly-wooded slopes of the Knott – a limestone headland which stretches along the shore of the bay. Until the 19th century Arnside was a local port which traded in slate but the building of the viaduct hastened the silting up of the estuary. Today the town is a modest holiday resort with visitor numbers boosted by surfers keen to ride the Arnside Bore which can produce waves half a metre high at spring high tides.

HARTSOP

The small village of Hartsop lies in Patterdale (above), in what was once a royal hunting ground, now home to deer, red squirrels and badgers. The village is overlooked by the two fells of Brocks Crag and Hartsop Dodd. It is a popular starting point for walkers climbing Helvellyn and the High Street Fell, named after the Roman road which crosses its summit. The Roman road was part of a route which ran all the way to the coastal town of Ravenglass via Ambleside and the fort at Hardknott, high above Eskdale.

AMBLESIDE

On the northern shores of Windermere, Ambleside (right) has been one of the most important centres in the Lake District since Victorian times. To the north is Scandale Fell, the source of Scandale Beck that skirts the upper reaches of the town. Old Bridge House, built on top of the packhorse bridge over Stock Beck to avoid land tax, now belongs to the National Trust. Overlooking Ambleside is Orrest Head. This easily reached hill is 784ft (239m) high and gives travellers from the south their first breathtaking views of the Lake District.

RYDAL WATER AND GRASMERE

The Lakeland poet William Wordsworth has long been associated with Rydal Water, seen here in the foreground, (above) with the village and lake of Grasmere (behind). At the western end of Rydal Water there is a rocky outcrop which was one of the poet's favourite viewpoints. It is now known as Wordsworth's Seat. From 1813 until his death in 1850, Wordsworth made his home at Rydal Mount on a hillside overlooking the lake. The Wordsworth Museum in Grasmere is attached to Dove Cottage, where the poet lived for nine years from 1799. He lies buried in the cemetery in St Oswald's parish church in the village.

THIRLMERE

Thirlmere (right) was once two smaller lakes, but such was the need for water at the end of the 19th century that Manchester Corporation bought the lakes and created one large reservoir. During this process a dam was built at the northern end and the two small hamlets of Armboth and Wythburn were submerged. North-West Water now owns Thirlmere and has recently opened the area to the public.

PATTERDALE

The village of Patterdale lies in the valley (right) of the same name. It is the starting point for walks into the surrounding hills including the Striding Edge path up Helvellyn. The renowned hill-walker and author Alfred Wainwright considered this his favourite valley in the Lakes because of its relatively unspoilt nature. To the south of Patterdale, the road to Ambleside leads over the Kirkstone Pass. At the top of the pass sits the Kirkstone Pass Inn, one of the highest pubs in England.

HELVELLYN

At a height of 3117ft (950m), Helvellyn (below) is the third highest mountain both in the Lake District and in England. It is one of only four peaks in the Lake District that rise above 3000ft (915m). To the west lies Thirlmere; to the east Patterdale. Although the approach to the summit is quite challenging, the actual summit area is quite flat. In 1926 John Leeming and Bert Hinkler managed to land a plane and take off again, thereby recording the first ever mountain-top landing of an aircraft.

STRIDING EDGE

The most dramatic ridge in the Lake District, Striding Edge (right) forms part of the south-eastern route to Helvellyn. It starts at a point called the Hole in the Wall, at a height of 2296ft (700m) and stretches for over a mile up to the summit plateau. With crags and scree falling away either side of the main arête, Striding Edge is a notorious accident spot for unwary walkers and scramblers.

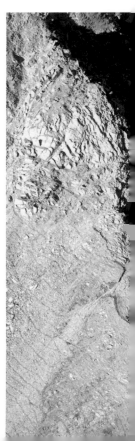

St Sunday Crag

Sometimes called the "Ullswater Fell", the rounded shape of St Sunday Crag (below) is a distinctive feature in Patterdale in the eastern fells. It is the highest point on the north-eastern ridge of Fairfield, soaring above the valleys of Deepdale and Grisedale and offering splendid views over Ullswater. St Sunday Crag lies on Alfred Wainwright's popular Coast to Coast Walk – a distance of 190 miles (306km) from St Bees Head on the west coast of Cumbria through the Lake District National Park, the Yorkshire Dales National Park and the North York Moors National Park to Robin Hood's Bay on the east Yorkshire coast. It takes the average walker 10-12 days to complete the trek.

Ullswater

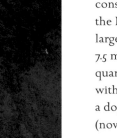

Ullswater (above and right) is often considered the most beautiful of the English lakes. It is the second largest lake in the Lake District at 7.5 miles (12km) long and three-quarters of a mile (1200m) wide, with three distinct bends that give it a dog-leg shape. Since 1855 steamers (now diesel-powered) have connected the main centres on the lake: Glenridding to the south, Pooley Bridge to the north-east and Howtown halfway between. Tourists particularly love this service as they can take a boat between Glenridding and Howtown and then walk back along one of the most popular and scenic low-level paths in the Lake District.

PART EIGHT
NORTH-EAST ENGLAND

Many people consider the north-east to be the friendliest of England's nine official regions. It is certainly full of natural beauty, with a dramatic coastline and thriving cities. The term Geordie is widely applied to the people who live here, though some would say its strict definition is someone who lives in Newcastle-upon-Tyne. You hear the Geordie dialect across a large part of the region. To the north is the bleak beauty of the legendary Hadrian's Wall and Northumberland, England's least populated county. Further south there is a new buzz about the bustling cities such as Newcastle, Gateshead, Sunderland and Durham with their trendy shopping centres, busy nightlife and growing cultural importance.

NEWCASTLE – BRIDGING THE TYNE

Both Newcastle and its close neighbour of Gateshead across the river have a long history of shipbuilding and heavy industry. Now most of this has gone and the area is utilising its past history in its regenerated buildings and riverside developments, many of which are arts-related. There has been a bridge at this point across the river Tyne since Roman times. Today there are no less than seven, from the Redheugh roadbridge (right, foreground), then the King Edward VII railway bridge and the Queen Elizabeth II metro bridge. Next is the High Level combined road and railway bridge and just visible behind is the 1876 Swing Bridge. Behind it soars the Tyne Bridge, a fine compression arch

suspended-deck bridge, modelled on the Sydney Harbour Bridge. Finally the Millennium Bridge for cyclists and pedestrians, which opened in 2001. Nicknamed the "Blinking Eye", it tilts to allow small ships and boats to pass beneath.

Echoing the curves of the nearby bridges, the shell-shaped Sage Gateshead (above) opened in 2004 as the quayside's latest addition to the skyline. It is Sir Norman Foster's first building dedicated to the performing arts and is home to the Northern Sinfonia orchestra. Just beyond the Sage and the Millennium Bridge is the Baltic Centre for Contemporary Art, converted from the former Baltic Flour Mills.

St James' Park

Football has been played at St James' Park (above) since 1880. In 1892 Newcastle East End joined forces with Newcastle West End to form Newcastle United Football Club and this has been their home ground ever since. In their distinctive black and white strip, the team is known as the Magpies to their fans. St James' Park is the third biggest club ground in England after Manchester United's Old Trafford and Arsenal's Emirates Stadium. The stadium dominates the area just to the north of the city centre; under the ownership of Sir John Hall, it was completely redeveloped in the late 1990s with all-seater stands. The stadium is a perfect venue for large-scale concerts – visiting stars have included the Rolling Stones and Rod Stewart.

THE ANGEL OF THE NORTH

Taller than four double-decker buses and with wings almost as wide as those of a Jumbo jet, Antony Gormley's Angel of the North (above) attracts more than 150,000 visitors annually. The statue on a hillside outside Gateshead was completed in 1998; 65ft (20m) high and 175ft (54m) wide, it can be seen by drivers on the A1 and passengers on the east coast railway line. At first the Angel was controversial, but it is now very popular and has been classed as an "Icon of England" along with cricket and fish and chips!

ST MARY'S LIGHTHOUSE

For 86 years from 1898 St Mary's Lighthouse (below) operated to mark a hazardous stretch of coastline to the north of Whitley Bay. Reached by a short causeway which is covered at high tide, the lighthouse and the former lighthouse-keepers' cottages are now a popular visitor centre, open according to tidal conditions. Energetic visitors can climb the lighthouse's 137 steps to be rewarded with spectacular views along the coast. Down below you can explore the rockpools, beach and wetland habitat of the surrounding nature reserve.

SUNDERLAND

When still a small fishing village Sunderland (above) at the mouth of the river Wear was granted a charter in 1179. By the 19th century it had become a major trading port. It was the first British port to be hit by the Indian cholera epidemic of 1831, which went on to kill 32,000 people across Britain. Sunderland gained

city status in 1992 and today new industries such as Nissan line the banks of the river. Upstream from the seafront the ultra-modern National Glass Centre offers visitors and craftspeople a chance to explore contemporary glassmaking. Every July the Sunderland International Airshow,

Europe's largest free air event, attracts 1.2m visitors. In recent years Sunderland AFC has had a tenuous hold on a place in the FA Premier League. The football team, known locally as the Black Cats, can trace its history back to 1879. In 1997 when they moved from Roker Park to the

spectacular Stadium of Light (foreground) on the banks of the river Wear the rock band Status Quo played at the opening match. Sunderland still holds the record for the highest scoring away win in England's top division: 9-1 in a local derby against Newcastle United on December 5 1908.

CHEVIOT HILLS

The rolling wooded Cheviot Hills (above) straddle the Scottish Borders and the county of Northumberland. The hills formed from an extinct volcano; when the lava cooled it produced distinctive pink rocks. They are criss-crossed by bridleways, popular with mountain-bikers. The aptly-named Windy Gyle is the only hill with its top on the border proper. The highest hill is the 2674ft (815m) Cheviot, just over a mile south of the Scottish border. The Cheviots form the most northerly range of the Pennines, the range of hills that form England's backbone. The Pennine Way stretches 267 miles (429km) from Edale in the Peak District, through the Yorkshire Dales and Northumberland National Parks to its end at Kirk Yetholm.

HADRIAN'S WALL

The Roman Emperor Hadrian ordered a great wall (right) built of stone and turf to be erected after his visit to Britain in 122AD. At 13-15ft high and extending more than 70 miles (114km) west from Wallsend on the river Tyne to the Solway Firth, it was a huge effort of construction. The forts, temples, milecastles and turrets were manned by more than 10,000 troops. For more than 250 years it succeeded in defending Roman England from the marauding Picts (the early Scots). Hadrian's Wall does not mark the modern border but is located entirely in England between nine miles (15km) and 68 miles (110km) south of the Scottish border. It is a World Heritage Site and one of northern England's most popular attractions.

HOUSESTEADS ROMAN FORT

Halfway along Hadrian's Wall stands Housesteads (left), the Roman fort of *Vercovicium* built in 124AD. The fort's layout is rather unusual: its northern wall forms part of Hadrian's Wall, whereas all other forts extended into Barbarian territory. The fort is on a high ridge, and the views are remarkable. Its magnificent ruins include one of the best-kept stone latrines of Roman Britain.

LAMBLEY VIADUCT

The South Tyne river meanders from its source, south of Garrigill, to Warden Rock. There it meets the North Tyne and becomes the river Tyne. The 23 mile (36.5km) South Tyne Trail was set up in 2004 for walkers and cyclists. A feature on the trail is Lambley Viaduct (below) 110ft (33.5m) above the river. Dating from 1852, the viaduct was part of the Newcastle and Carlisle Railway and closed in 1976.

MIDDLESBROUGH

In 1801 Middlesbrough (left) was a small hamlet of four farmhouses and 25 inhabitants. Nearly 30 years later Quaker businessmen set up a port here for the north-east's coal. By the end of the 19th century the iron and steelworks on the banks of the river Tees employed 6,000 men. These are still important industries in the area today.

The 35,100 capacity all-seater Riverside Stadium opened in 1995 on the site of a former petro-chemical storage facility. It is home to Middlesbrough FC, whose nickname is the Boro. The Transporter Bridge (right) between Middlesbrough and Port Clarence dates from 1911 and is one of only two still working in Britain today.

HARTLEPOOL

Founded in the 7th century, Hartlepool (below) derives its name from the Old English *heort-ieg* meaning "hart (stag) island" and *pol* meaning "pool". Over the centuries, Hartlepool developed into an important town and harbour. Heavy industry arrived during the 19th century and by 1913 the town boasted 43 shipping companies with 236 ships. In 2010 the town will serve as the finishing line for the 125 sail training ships taking part in the Tall Ships Race.

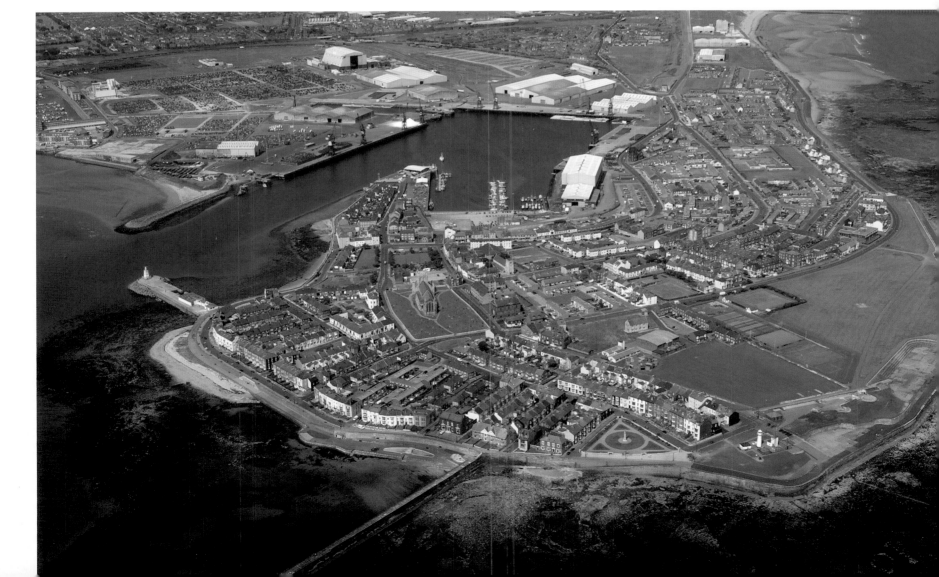

PART NINE

WALES

Few countries have such a dramatic combination of mountain scenery, beautiful coastline, pretty villages and vibrant cities all within a relatively compact area. The ring of castles on the north and north-west coast are testament to the country's turbulent history. In the south the combination of coal and steel production powered the Industrial Revolution and quickened the growth of cities such as Cardiff and Swansea. In 2002 the Welsh Assembly was created – a powerful symbol of the resurgence of Wales.

MENAI STRAIT

Separating the island of Anglesey from the Welsh mainland, the Menai Strait (below) extends for some 14 miles (23 km). At its widest it is two miles (3km) across. The two famous bridges span the swirling waters where the strait narrows to just 600ft (180m). This stretch, known locally as the Swellies or Pwll Ceris, is full of whirlpools and sharp rocks. Thomas Telford's elegant iron suspension bridge opened on January 30 1826 and reduced the journey time from London to Holyhead from 36 to 27 hours. Robert Stephenson's Britannia Bridge which opened on March 5 1850 started life as a railway bridge but was rebuilt in 1970 after a disastrous fire. The current bridge has two decks which combine road and rail. It carries the railway line on its lower deck and a single carriageway of the A55 on its upper deck.

HOLY ISLAND

Holy Island (left) nestles beside its larger sister island of Anglesey and is connected to it by a bridge. The island's maritime importance dates back to 3AD when the Romans built a watchtower on Holyhead Mountain, the island's highest point. Packet boats have crossed the Irish Sea from the port of Holyhead since 1573, and today the ferry still runs to Ireland. South Stack Island (foreground), with its lighthouse, is popular with birdwatchers. The nearby cliffs host more than 4,000 nesting birds during the breeding season.

PENRHYN BAY

Sheltered from the east by the Little Orme headland, Penrhyn Bay (below) is thought to be the location of one of King Arthur's castles. In the 19th century the Pennant family, who had made their fortunes from the slate trade and their estates in the West Indies, built the dramatic Penrhyn Castle just west of Bangor. Now owned by the National Trust, the castle has a Norman-style exterior and attractive gardens. In the 20th century Penrhyn Bay developed into a sought-after suburb of its neighbour Llandudno, the "queen of Welsh resorts". The wide sweep of sand and shingle of Llandudno Bay stretches for two miles in a graceful curve from Little Orme to Great Orme. Llandudno Pier was once visited by paddle steamers from Liverpool carrying passengers for their annual holidays in this splendid resort. Each year in early May Llandudno celebrates its heritage with a three-day Victorian carnival.

CONWY

The classic walled town of Conwy (above) is guarded by 22 towers, and is dominated by its dark-stoned castle, now a World Heritage Site. Edward 1 built this fortress on the Conwy estuary in just six years, starting in 1283. It became one of his "iron ring" of castles, built to contain the Welsh. There are three parallel bridges crossing the estuary. Robert Stephenson's tubular railway bridge is furthest from the sea and was designed with mock fortifications at each end. Two further bridges for road traffic included the Conwy Suspension Bridge built by Thomas Telford in 1826. These days, the suspension bridge is the preserve of pedestrians, and all road traffic now crosses the river by tunnel.

COLWYN BAY

The resort of Colwyn Bay (right) sits beautifully between the sea and the Pwllycrochan Woods on the north Welsh coast. It is linked by a long promenade to its sister communities of Rhos-on-Sea and Old Colwyn. Jutting out into the sea is Victoria Pier, which was officially opened on June 1 1900. After a chequered history the pier fell into disrepair and was closed to the public in 1991. It is now privately owned and re-opened in 2004 with a continuing programme of repair and development that aims to restore its 1930s style. In 1170 the Welsh prince Madoc ap Owain Gwynedd is said to have sailed from Rhos-on-Sea and discovered America, some 300 years before Columbus.

GREAT ORME

The castellated lighthouse at Great Orme (left) was built in 1862 and is now a magnificent Victorian-style guesthouse. It is perched on the edge of the headland of Great Orme, overlooking Llandudno. It is possible to take a trip up to the summit (679ft/207m) on Britain's only remaining cable-operated street tramway, opened in 1901. Great Orme is managed as a country park and has been designated a special area of conservation and a site of special scientific interest. The name "Orme" is thought to derive from an old Norse word for worm or sea serpent. On the other side of Llandudno is Little Orme, a smaller version of Great Orme.

Snowdon

Yr Wyddfa, or Snowdon in English, is the highest mountain in England and Wales at 3560ft (1085m). The botanist Thomas Johnson made the first ever recorded ascent of Snowdon in 1639. Today the mountain draws many thousands of visitors for some of the most extensive views in Britain. On exceptionally clear days you can see Ireland, Scotland, England and Wales, as well as 24 counties, 29 lakes and 17 islands.

Snowdon's six ridges each have their own special character. Those to the north and east are steep and rocky, and those to the south and west are grassy but more remote. There are seven main routes on foot to reach the summit of Snowdon (right). They range from the easiest, the Llanberis Path or Tourist Path, to the toughest, the Snowdon Horseshoe (top right).

Most walkers take the Miners Track which skirts Llyn Glaslyn or Blue Lake at a height of 2200ft (670m).

A more leisurely way to reach the summit is aboard the Snowdon Mountain Railway which opened in 1896. This is Britain's only public rack and pinion railway. It climbs over 1000ft (305m) from Llanberis at an average speed of five miles per hour to the summit station at 3493ft (1065m). When the railway first opened, a hotel was built at the summit terminus but this was replaced in the 1930s by a restaurant. The restaurant had become so dilapidated by the end of the 20th century that Prince Charles described it as "the highest slum in Wales". Visitors will now be relieved to find that a new visitor centre opened in 2008.

CAERNARFON

At the western end of the Menai Strait, Caernarfon is the largest Welsh-speaking community in Wales. But the legacy of English rule is evident. The magnificent castle (above) with its 13 towers was built by Edward I in 1283, as a seat of power and a symbol of English dominance. Edward I proclaimed his son the first Prince of Wales at the castle in 1301. The investiture of a new Prince of Wales, held at Caernarfon Castle, is a relatively new idea, conceived by the local MP, David Lloyd George, and first held in 1911. The ceremony was again held on July 1 1969 at Caernarfon when Queen Elizabeth II invested her son Charles as Prince of Wales.

PWLLHELI

The market town of Pwllheli (right) is considered the unofficial capital of the Llyn Peninsula. The town was given its charter as a borough by the Black Prince in 1355 and a weekly market is still held every Wednesday. The town is mainly Welsh-speaking and the Welsh political party Plaid Cymru was founded here in 1925.

The name Pwllheli means saltwater basin. The town has two beaches, South Beach and Glan-y-mor, and has developed into a popular seaside resort. The impressive marina is the only sheltered harbour in the north of Cardigan Bay and offers deep-water moorings for about 400 boats.

PORTMEIRION

The architect Clough Williams-Ellis built Portmeirion (right) to show how a naturally beautiful place could be developed without spoiling it. The result was a unique village of about 50 buildings built in two stages: from 1925 to 1939 in the Arts & Crafts style, and from 1954 to 1975 in the more classical Palladian style. Many of the second phase buildings were salvaged from demolition sites, which meant that Portmeirion was often called "a home for fallen buildings". Today the village, with its elegant hotel (foreground), is used as holiday accommodation. Portmeirion Pottery, established by Clough Williams-Ellis' daughter and her husband in 1960, is based in Stoke-on-Trent.

BARMOUTH

The seaside resort of Barmouth is situated in one of the loveliest locations in Wales at the mouth of the Mawddach estuary (above). Pedestrians pay a small toll to cross Barmouth Bridge, a railway viaduct. To the seaward side of the bridge a ferry takes visitors to join the 15-inch narrow gauge railway to Fairbourne. Every year teams leave Barmouth harbour for Fort William on the Three Peaks yacht race. They sail, run and cycle, climbing to the top of the highest points in Wales, England and Scotland – Snowdon, Scafell Pike and Ben Nevis.

ABERYSTWYTH

The university town of Aberystwyth stands at the mouth of the river Ystwyth almost at the centre of Cardigan Bay. Its castle, built by the Welsh leader Llywelyn ap Gruffydd in the 13th century, ranked among the greatest in Wales for 100 years. It decayed rapidly however, attacked by successive English and Welsh armies and eroded by the surrounding sea and slowly fell into ruin. Situated on the north shore is the grand Old College Building, bought in 1872 to establish the University College of Wales. Today Aberystwyth is also home to the National Library of Wales.

HARLECH

Seemingly growing out of the rock on which it sits and guards Snowdonia, Harlech Castle (below) dominates the surrounding area. Edward I began building it in 1283 as one of his "iron ring" of fortresses to subdue the Welsh. Today the sea has retreated but the castle's massive inner walls and towers still stand almost to their full height. This is a truly formidable castle built in just seven years by a military architect with strategic foresight. Attackers faced daunting challenges: a sheer cliff-face rising from the sea and, on the landward side, the massive twin-towered gatehouse and concentric outer and inner walls. The Welsh leader Owain Glyndŵr succeeded in capturing the castle in 1404, and held a parliament there. Four years later Prince Henry (later Henry V) took it after a long siege. During the Wars of the Roses in 1468 its occupants surrendered after a seven-year siege – they were only able to resist for so long because they got supplies by sea. The siege inspired the ever-popular marching song *Men of Harlech*.

TENBY

The popular seaside resort of Tenby (left) situated on Carmarthen Bay in Pembrokeshire in west Wales, can trace its roots back to a Viking settlement, but today is a popular seaside resort. Just offshore, and linked to Tenby by a beach at low tide, is St Catherine's Island, known locally as St Catherine's Rock. It is home to a fort built in 1870 to protect Pembroke Dock.

WORM'S HEAD

Worm's Head (below) is shaped like a giant sea serpent, which inspired Viking invaders to name it *Wurm* (meaning "dragon"). The headland forms the most westerly point of the Gower Peninsula – and the most photographed. The mile-long promontory is joined to the mainland by a rocky causeway, which is only exposed for two-and-a-half hours at low tide. Each part has its own name: the large flat-topped Inner Head, the natural rock bridge called Devil's Bridge, Low Neck and the Outer Head, a breeding ground for kittiwakes, herring gulls, guillemots and razorbills.

SWANSEA

The second largest city in Wales lies on the south coast at the mouth of the river Tawe, and is considered the gateway to the Gower Peninsula. Although it was a centre of heavy industry in the 18th and 19th centuries, Swansea (right) was only granted city status in 1969. Its recently regenerated dock areas, the Marina and Maritime Quarter, house many high-tech industries and also the new £30m National Waterfront Museum. The most famous literary figure in Wales, Dylan Thomas, was born in Swansea in 1914 and lived there until the age of 20. The Dylan Thomas Festival is held annually in the city and runs from October 27 (the date of the writer's birth) until November 9 (the date of his death).

PORT TALBOT

This was once a small port and market town called Aberafan, or Aberavon in English, which belonged to the medieval Lords of Afan. The Talbot family re-named it Port Talbot in the middle of the 19th century. Built along the eastern rim of Swansea Bay in Glamorgan in south Wales, Port Talbot (above) is today a busy industrial town and harbour. The town is dominated by the Port Talbot Steelworks, originally part of British Steel, subsequently Corus, and which now belong to Tata Steel of India. The film director Ridley Scott has been quoted as saying that the sight of the steelworks at night inspired the dark, gigantic buildings in his film *Blade Runner*.

RHONDDA VALLEY

The view above is close to Porth, "the gateway to the Rhondda", which lies at the entrance to the two Rhondda valleys, the Rhondda Fach (little Rhondda) and the Rhondda Fawr (large Rhondda). This was once a sparsely populated area of great natural beauty, but the arrival of the railway in the middle of the 19th century brought the coal industry. Porth was one of the first districts in the Rhondda to experience industrialisation on a large scale. Coalmining was to dominate the lives of the people and the landscape of the Rhondda valley for the next 150 years. However, when British Coal was privatised in the 1980s many of the mines were closed. Today the story of coal is re-told at the site of a former colliery at Trehafod, now known as the nearby Rhondda Heritage Park, and which is one of the top visitor and heritage attractions in south Wales. Interestingly, back in 1944, some 4,000 American soldiers were billeted in the Rhondda Fawr in preparation for the D-Day landings in northern France.

MONMOUTH

The Romans knew Monmouth (above) as *Blestium*, one of a network of forts in this part of south-east Wales. The town lies at the confluence of the Monnow and Wye rivers. Monnow Bridge, built in 1272, has the only remaining medieval bridge gatehouse in Britain. Henry V was born in 1387 in the Norman castle in the town. The Great Castle House built from its ruins now houses the castle and regimental museums.

ABERGAVENNY

The gateway to south Wales, Abergavenny (right) also dates from the Roman era. Its fine motte and bailey castle witnessed a massacre in 1175 when the local baron, William de Braose, murdered local Welsh chieftains. The town's reputation is much friendlier today! A museum in the castle's restored keep and hunting lodge tells the story of the castle as well as the local area from prehistoric times.

PEN Y FAN

At 2907ft (886m) Pen y Fan (left) is the highest mountain in south Wales. It is situated in the Brecon Beacons, Wales' third national park which was established in 1957. The park gets its name from the ancient custom of lighting beacons (signal fires) on the mountains to warn of impending attacks by the English. Formed of glaciated old red sandstone, Pen y Fan has the reputation of being the most dangerous peak in Wales. Its rapidly changing weather conditions have led to a number of casualties over the years, both novice walkers and highly trained soldiers.

CARDIFF

A small town until the early 19th century, Cardiff (below) became a city in 1905 and the capital of Wales in 1955. During the 19th century, Cardiff's port – known as Tiger Bay – was one of the world's busiest, exporting coal from the surrounding valleys to destinations around the world. Today, Wales' largest city is a major centre of culture, sport, finance and business services; the magnificent new building, designed by Sir Richard Rogers for the National Assembly for Wales, houses the recently devolved government, built close to Cardiff Bay. Nearby is the Wales Millennium Centre, a stunning arts and entertainment complex. In the city centre is the Millennium Stadium, the national stadium of Wales. When it opened in 1999 its retractable roof was unique. Rugby, football and speedway fans flock to the stadium for key sporting events and it is also a popular venue for rock concerts.

THE SEVERN RIVER CROSSINGS

Thomas Telford had dreamed for years of building a bridge to span the Severn estuary. But it was not until 1966 that this dream became a reality when the original Severn Bridge (foreground, right) was opened. This elegant suspension bridge, an icon of Wales, is 5240ft (1597m) long and it carried all the M4 traffic across the Severn estuary. The bridge followed the exact route of the old ferry crossing between Aust in south Gloucestershire to Beachley in Monmouthshire. By 1986 the volume of traffic was such that a second crossing was needed and work started on it some three miles further downstream in 1992. Four years later, the Prince of Wales inaugurated the Second Severn Crossing. It is just over three miles (5km) long and now carries the M4 in a more direct route from England to Wales. Tolls are charged on both crossings – but only when travelling west.

NEWPORT

The third largest city in Wales, Newport (right) straddles the banks of the river Usk. The remarkable Transporter Bridge (foreground) opened in 1906 and is one of only eight in the world. Its French designer, Ferdinand Arnodin, had to be innovative because the river banks are very low but the river is tidal. He came up with a platform suspended from a horizontal beam 177ft (54m) above the roadway. The platform can take six cars and 120 foot passengers and travels the 592ft (181m) between the towers at a speed of 10ft (3m) per second. The bow-string arch of the City Bridge (right of picture) which opened in 2004, is widely considered to symbolise the best in British bridge engineering.

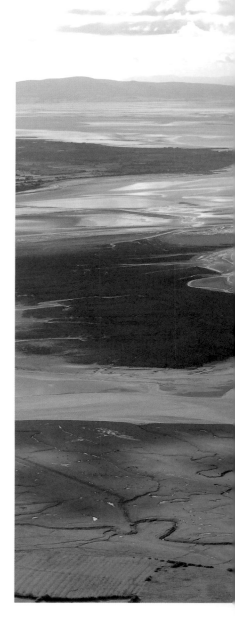

PART TEN

SCOTLAND

There is more to Scotland than Edinburgh, Glasgow and the Highlands. There are 162 islands with Unst in the Shetlands the most northerly inhabited Scottish isle – it is nearer to Bergen in Norway than to Aberdeen. Rivalry between the Scots and the English is intense, particularly when it comes to sport. It is the legacy of both countries' history: Scotland is littered with battle sites where Scots and English troops fought for control over the centuries. The Acts of Union of 1707 finally united the two peoples under the Kingdom of Great Britain. With devolution in 1998 Scotland regained political control over its education, health and other regional issues. The magnificent new Parliament building in Edinburgh, designed by the Catalan architect Enric Miralles, opened in 2004.

CAMPBELTOWN

Kinlochkilkerran (meaning "head of the loch by the church of St Kieran") was the original Gaelic name for Campbeltown (above). By the time the Earl of Argyll, the chief of the Campbell clan, changed its name in the 17th century, the town had become a centre for ship-building, fishing and Scotch whisky. There used to be 34 distilleries producing single malts in Campbeltown, but today there are only two: Springbank and Glen Scotia. In 2002 a memorial garden to the late Linda McCartney was opened in Campbeltown.

MULL OF KINTYRE

The southern tip of the Kintyre peninsula, the Mull of Kintyre (right) was made famous in the song by ex-Beatle Paul McCartney and Denny Laine, his fellow songwriter. Its Gaelic name is *Maol Ceanntìre*. The word *maol* is used in this part of south-west Scotland for the bare tip of a peninsula or promontory. A narrow isthmus at Tarbet at its northern end is the only thing that prevents this 30-mile (48km) long stretch of land from becoming an island. When the weather is clear you can see Northern Ireland and Ailsa Craig.

SOLWAY FIRTH

The border between England and Scotland was established in law by the Treaty of York in 1237 and is one of the oldest in the world. The Solway Firth (left) forms the western edge of the border, and stretches from St Bees Head near Whitehaven in Cumbria to the Mull of Galloway in Dumfries and Galloway.

AILSA CRAIG

Appearing out of the mist, the conical shape of Ailsa Craig (below) rises 1114ft (340m) from the waters of the Firth of Clyde, about 10 miles (16km) west of the town of Girvan. The uninhabited island is home to a huge number of gannets and a growing colony of puffins. Granite from the island has traditionally been used to make the stones used in the Scottish sport of curling.

GLASGOW

Glasgow's Gaelic name was *Glaschu*, meaning "dear green place". Today it is Scotland's largest city, but its history goes back to the Celtic Druids. In the 6th century St Kentigern established a church where the city's cathedral now stands. In 1450 James II made Glasgow a royal burgh in all but name and Glasgow Green (above right, foreground) became its first public park.

After the Acts of Union in the 1700s, Glasgow started to develop commercial links with the rest of the British Empire trading in tobacco, sugar and cotton. Shipbuilding gained importance and by the end of the 19th century Glasgow was considered the second city of the Empire. Most of the world's locomotives and ships were made on the Clyde, and many of the Cunard liners including the *Queen Mary*, *Queen Elizabeth*, *Queen Elizabeth II* and the former royal yacht *Britannia*.

The centre of modern Glasgow spreads from Kingston Bridge (which carries the M8 motorway over the river), past the central railway bridges to Albert Bridge near Glasgow Green. The city will host the 2014 Commonwealth Games.

21ST CENTURY GLASGOW

After the Second World War Glasgow's traditional industries such as shipbuilding were no longer viable and the city went into a slump. But a conscious cultural renaissance was rewarded with the status of European Capital of Culture in 1990 and Glasgow is now a dynamic centre for business and tourism. The former Queen's Dock, on the north bank of the Clyde, is now the Scottish Exhibition and Conference Centre (left). Part of this complex is the Armadillo – more formally called the Clyde Auditorium – a 3,000-seater concert venue which opened in 1997. Across the river the Glasgow Science Centre (right) is a major tourist attraction. Its circular IMAX cinema (Scotland's first, and only, such cinema) opened in 2000 and has a screen larger than a five-a-side football pitch. Next door is the Science Mall with three floors of over 300 hands-on scientific exhibits and the ScottishPower Space Theatre planetarium. This gleaming titanium building opened in 2001, as did the nearby 400ft (122m) Glasgow Tower. The tower is unique – the whole slender building above ground is shaped like an aerofoil and can rotate through 360° to minimise wind resistance.

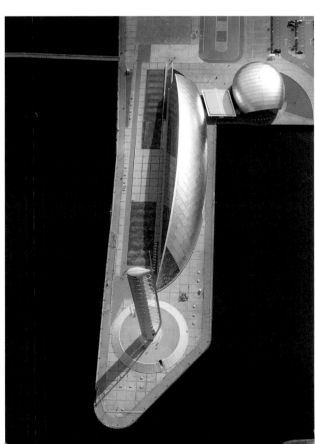

LOCH LOMOND

As the cloud lifts, the waters of Loch Lomond (left) are revealed. This is the UK's largest stretch of fresh water, 24 miles (39km) long by five miles (8km) wide. There are about 38 islands in the loch, which is overlooked by the 3194ft (974m) mountain Ben Lomond.

The loch is the jewel in the crown of the Loch Lomond and Trossachs National Park which was created in 2002 and contains some of Scotland's finest scenery. The park boasts no fewer than 20 Munros – mountains over 3000ft (914m).

The West Highland Way long-distance path heads up the eastern shore of the loch. It runs for 95 miles (152km) from Milngavie north of Glasgow to Fort William.

LOCH ETIVE

The fjord-like Loch Etive (left) doglegs almost 20 miles (32km) from the foot of Glen Etive to the open waters of the Firth of Lorn. For most of its length there is no road and little habitation, so the area is popular with walkers and climbers. At Connel, at the mouth of the loch, the occasional phenomenon known as the Falls of Lora attracts white-water canoeing enthusiasts.

BEN NEVIS

Britain's highest mountain, known locally as the Ben, is the 4406ft (1344m) Ben Nevis (below). It was first climbed in 1771 by the Edinburgh botanist, James Robertson. When the poet John Keats reached the summit 47 years later, he compared the experience of climbing the Ben to "mounting ten St Pauls without the convenience of a staircase". Today there are about 100,000 ascents a year, mostly via the pony track from Glen Nevis.

LOCH NESS

The home of Nessie, the famous but imaginary monster, Loch Ness (above) is the deepest of the Scottish lochs, and the second largest by surface area after Loch Lomond. It stretches about 23 miles (37km) between Fort Augustus in the south and Lochend in the north.

INVERNESS

Where the river Ness flows into the Moray Firth lies Inverness (left) the capital of the Scottish Highlands. The town hosts the annual Inverness Highland Games in July. Events include tossing the caber, a heavy tree trunk 16ft (5m) long, and throwing the 22lb (10kg) Inverness Stone. All competitors must wear kilts.

TAY BRIDGES

The Tay Rail Bridge (foreground right) across the Firth of Tay is the second on the site and opened in 1887. The central section of the first bridge collapsed in a storm in 1879 with the loss of 75 lives. Further downstream, the Tay Road Bridge carries the A92 across the Firth.

URQUHART CASTLE

The early history of Urquhart Castle (left) on Loch Ness is unclear. It was captured by Edward I of England in 1296 and last saw action in 1689 when a garrison of supporters of William and Mary fought off troops loyal to James II. Three years later the castle was blown up. The ruins are now owned by the National Trust for Scotland.

ABERDEEN

Scotland's third city, Aberdeen (below) is known as the Granite City and the Oil Capital of Europe. Much of the city was built in the early 19th century using local granite. In the 1970s the town boomed with the discovery of North Sea oil, and today it has the world's second largest heliport and an important harbour to service offshore oilrigs. Ferry services operate from Aberdeen to Orkney and Shetland.

EDINBURGH

Capital of Scotland since 1437, Edinburgh has been the seat of the new Scottish Parliament since devolution in 1998. As a World Heritage Site it attracts 13m tourists each year, making it the UK's second most visited city.

Edinburgh Castle (below) vies with Kelvingrove Art Gallery and Museum in Glasgow for the title of Scotland's most visited attraction. The castle dominates the city from its perch on Castle Rock. Most of it dates from the 16th century, though St Margaret's Chapel was built in the 12th century and is Edinburgh's oldest building. Every day except Sunday, the one o'clock gun booms over the city, a practice originally begun to provide a reliable time check for ships in the Firth of Forth.

The arena with the blue seating next to the castle is used by military bands for the Edinburgh Military Tattoo. This is part of the three-week Edinburgh International Festival held in August every year. Alongside the main festival's programme of classical music, theatre and opera, the Edinburgh Festival Fringe showcases alternative and experimental works.

Across the Princes St Gardens runs Princes Street, one of Edinburgh's main shopping streets.

The King George IV bridge (right) is an elevated roadway that crosses the city's other famous street, the Royal Mile, which runs from the castle down to Holyrood House. Up by the fork are the Royal Museum and Museum of Scotland, where you can see the remains of Dolly the sheep, the first mammal to be cloned.

FORTH BRIDGES

There was already a ferry operating in the 12th century across the Firth of Forth (above) between Queensferry and North Queensferry. By 1760 it was Scotland's busiest service but it was slow and sometimes dangerous despite improvements to the piers. The ferry was finally replaced in 1964 by the Forth Road Bridge (foreground).

Just over 1.5 miles (2.5km) long from end to end, the Forth Road Bridge was Europe's longest suspension bridge when it opened. Two 512ft (156m) tall towers support its 3300ft (1005m) central span. Until 2007 drivers had to pay a toll when travelling northwards but the Scottish Parliament abolished all remaining bridge tolls.

The Forth Railway Bridge was opened in 1890. It was one of the world's first steel bridges, requiring 54,000 tonnes of steel and 4000 men to drive home 6.5 million rivets! Painting of the 45acre (18ha) surface was a never-ending job, but technology has come to the rescue of the bridge's maintenance team: the paint used today is designed to last 20 years.

CALLENDAR HOUSE

Originally just a stone tower dating from 1345, by 1878 Callendar House (left) had expanded into the French-style chateau with its imposing 300ft (91m) frontage we see today. It is set in extensive parkland in Falkirk. Mary Queen of Scots spent her early years here, and its history includes guests such as Oliver Cromwell, Bonnie Prince Charlie and Queen Victoria. Today Callendar House functions as a museum where the costumed staff bring history to life.